The City of Ely may be small in comparison with other cities, but it can look back on a history which has lasted for almost 1300 years. Although remote in its Fenland fastness it has been visited by men and women well-known in the pages of history. Canute, William the Conqueror, Hereward the Wake, Henry III, Edward III and Queen Phillipa, Oliver Cromwell, the Prince Regent and many more. The events of this long period have been recorded, not only in words but in stones, and although the Author has drawn on many sources of information he has tried to include only such things as he could verify from personal observation of the buildings concerned. Sufficient has been said to give the reader a picture of the events of interest during thirteen centuries and if further detail is required the Bibliography will guide the reader in his researches. Behind the story he will be able to detect the gradual change in the status and fortunes of the inhabitants and learn how, under a quiet exterior, an industrious and closely knit community lives to the full.

# THE STORY OF ELY

Plate XLII.

The Elevation of the South Side of Ely Cathedral, taken A.D. 1756.

F. Wise del.

P. S. Lambern sculp.

THE CATHEDRAL AS IT APPEARED IN 1756

*From Bentham's History and Antiquities of the Conventual
and Cathedral Church of Ely*

# THE STORY OF ELY
## AND ITS CATHEDRAL

BERNARD E. DORMAN
F.R.S.A.

EAST ANGLIAN MAGAZINE LTD.
6 Great Colman Street
Ipswich

1973

© *Bernard E. Dorman* 1973

*First published* 1945
*Reprinted* 1947
*Reprinted* 1968
*Revised and enlarged edition* 1973

PRINTED IN GREAT BRITAIN
*By W. Jefferson & Son Ltd.*
*Ely*

# Contents

# Illustrations

## Plans

## Foreword to the First Edition
## by the late Bishop Wynn

I AM very glad to be asked to write a Foreword to this book. Mr. Dorman has been faced with the hard task of selecting the important events of the long history of Ely and its Minster and has done his task admirably. Everyone passing Ely in the train or by road or visiting the city for a few hours cannot but feel the majesty and grandeur of the Norman Church: but anyone who lives in Ely soon finds that the Minster becomes a part of his life, just as from all points of the compass, he may see her towers rising above the Fens as they have risen for centuries.

EDWARD ELY.

THE BISHOP'S HOUSE,
ELY.
*June*, 1945.

# Preface to the First Edition

In his essay on Ely in the collection entitled *Hills and the Sea*, Mr. Hilaire Belloc concludes by saying, "No man lives in Ely for a year without beginning to write a book. I do not say that all are published, but I swear that all are begun." This is one of those books. I came to Ely eleven years ago and the idea of writing a book about the history of the place has been in my mind for a long time and some false starts were actually made. But it needed the spur provided by Mr. Bernard Cousin to make me complete this work, and I am grateful to him for providing it and for all he has done since in connection with its presentation to the public.

This volume is part of a scheme evolved by Mr. Cousin dealing with Ely past and present. It is hoped that it may be followed by a sequel entitled "Ely To-day," which is intended to consist of short articles presenting some of the civic, industrial, and cultural pursuits of the city and contributed by citizens who are engaged in these activities. Such a scheme should be of interest both to the youth of the city and their elders, although it is intended chiefly for the former. Knowledge of the present is not fully understood without knowledge of the past, and the combination of these two complementary factors is surely a sound means of fostering a love for one's own locality, which is the root upon which patriotism flourishes.

During the years I have known Ely Cathedral it has been a constant source of interest to me. Familiar as I am with all parts of the building, new details come to my notice with almost every visit. I should like to take this opportunity to thank Mr. W. Whetstone for the many things he has pointed out to me and for his ever-willing help when I have wanted to make observations for myself.

A considerable amount of research has been necessary to ascertain the facts given in this book. I particularly wish to acknowledge my debt to Canon D. J. Stewart's *Architectural History of Ely Cathedral*, which is probably the most complete book on the subject ever published in a convenient form. Some of Canon Stewart's statements have been challenged by Archdeacon Chapman in his *Sacrist Rolls of Ely*, a very valuable work which has been the authority used by later writers. I have also quoted from the Souvenir of the Bisexcentenary Celebrations of the Festival of St. Etheldreda, which was edited by Dean Merivale, Conybeare's *History of Cambridgeshire*, and other books mentioned in the text. Throughout I have tried to draw upon the most accurate sources. As space and simplicity have had to be considered, omissions must be considered to be intentional.  Much more could be said, and I hope that some day I may be able to present a fuller account of both the Cathedral and the City.

I wish to thank the Right Reverend the Lord Bishop of Ely for kindly contributing a foreword to this little book; also the Dean of Ely, the Reverend S. J. A. Evans, Colonel G. L. Archer, Major Fowler, Mr. F. H. Martin and Mr. S. C. Thompson for kind help and suggestions and for reading the typescript.  The first chapter owes much to both Major Fowler and Mr. Thompson, which could not be acknowledged in the text.  I also have to thank Mr. G. H. Tyndall for stimulating my interest in Ely when I first came to the City and for granting me permission to use his photographs to illustrate the book.  While this book was in the press Mr. Tyndall passed away.  He was a lover of Ely Cathedral and through his photographs and lectures made it better known than it would have been without him.

BERNARD E. DORMAN.

SOUTHSEA,
*January*, 1945.

## *Preface to the Revised Edition*

THIS book has been out of print for over twenty years and much has happened in the meantime.  I have taken the opportunity to make a number of corrections and additions to the text and to re-write and greatly expand the last chapter.  I hope that in doing so I have done justice to the great work of restoration which has taken place in the Cathedral and to improvements which have been made to the City in general.  It has also been possible to improve the presentation of the book, the first edition of which suffered from war-time restrictions on paper and other materials.

-B.E.D.

LITTLE MELTON,
NORWICH.
*November*, 1968.

# CHAPTER I
## The Beginnings of Ely

THE history of the City of Ely, as we shall see later, begins with the founding of the Abbey by Queen Etheldreda; but before recounting the part of the story which comes within historic times we will go back to the remote past and see how the countryside came to take its present shape. In later chapters, which deal with the defence of Ely and with the draining of the fens, the reader will find some slight knowledge of the physical characteristics of the district of assistance in understanding its changes and development. These physical characteristics have influenced the history of the district to a great extent.

Millions of years ago, at a period when the climate here was sub-tropical, a great sea covered the land where Ely now stands and left a deposit known as Kimmeridge clay. Fossils of prehistoric reptiles can still be found in this layer of clay which comes to the surface in the lower parts of the town. At a later period the land was again covered by a sea which left a deposit of greensand which comes to the surface in higher parts of the town. Above this layer is another deposit of much later date, consisting of Boulder Clay, which can be found at some of the highest points of the hill on which Ely stands, notably at the cemetery and near the water tower.

The Boulder Clay which has just been mentioned was deposited as a result of one of the Ice Ages, when many thousands of years ago, the area of ice round the North Pole extended much further south than it does now, at times covering most of the land which now forms the British Isles. Great glaciers crept slowly over the frozen land carrying rocks which were left lying on the ground, far from their native places, when the ice melted. The grinding action of the ice as it moved over rocks and earth formed a stony clay when the ice was gone. Sometimes large rocks became embedded in this clay which is the mixture known as Boulder Clay. Some of the Boulder Clay in Cambridgeshire contains stones which have been identified as having come from Yorkshire, Scotland, and even from Scandinavia.

The end of the Ice Age left the country in the Ely district in the form of hills and valleys. The hills, as we have seen in the case of Ely, were chiefly composed of very old deposits which had resisted the force of the glaciers. In course of time the valleys became

1

filled with alluvial deposits so that only the tops of the hills were left rising above a plain which became the Fenland of to-day. These hill-tops are the sites of the fen towns and villages, as, for instance, Ely, Littleport, Sutton and Haddenham. The rising ground at Barton Fields and the Little Downham ridge are capped by deposits of gravel due to the melting of the glaciers.

This plain, which bordered the Wash, was subject to a rising and falling action which is still supposed to be going on very slowly. During these changes the low-lying Fenland, as it became in time, was alternately subjected to flooding by fresh water brought down by the rivers, and to inundations by the sea. When the sea-water predominated, silt or buttery blue clay was deposited; the fresh water periods led to the formation of peat. The result of these changing conditions left the land in some places rather like a layer cake. Peat is formed by vegetation decaying in still water and consequently it makes a level surface. When dry it is a good form of fuel and much of it was cut and sold for this purpose until recent years. Most of what remains has been ploughed up and forms the rich black soil so familiar to the eye in the fen landscape. Owing to wastage due to drainage and cultivation all this peat fen soil will gradually disappear in course of time leaving its present subsoils at the surface which, with the exception of the silt and buttery blue clay, will probably prove poor for farming.

When the peat land was being formed, drier periods sometimes occurred which, while they lasted, enabled it to become thickly wooded. Tree trunks are still frequently discovered when dykes are dug, and the black logs often seen lying alongside fen drains are thousands of years old. Immersion in the water-logged soil has preserved them from decay.

Neolithic (New Stone Age about 2000 B.C.) and Bronze Age people, about 1500-500 B.C., occupied the margins and hills of the fens and, judging from the number of their weapons and tools that have been found under or in the peat, appear to have used the fens extensively as a hunting ground during dry periods.

During the earlier part of the Iron Age (about 500-100 B.C.), which followed the Bronze Age, the fens became less hospitable, and there are no traces of the people of those times except on the surrounding highlands. It was later in the Iron Age that the Romans came to Britain. They, or Romanized Britons, settled extensively on the firm silt land round the Wash which had recently been formed, and also along the banks of the lower reaches of the rivers which were composed of silt.

The courses of the rivers of Fenland in Romano-British times were very different from those of the straighter rivers of to-day which were made for drainage purposes. Some of the old rivers can be traced because their beds and banks are higher than the surrounding peat land which has wasted as a result of having the moisture drained out of it. The silt which formed the banks or levees of many of them has not wasted away and consequently remains more or less at its original level. These raised river beds are known as roddens. One fine example, which is the original course of the Little Ouse River, can be seen running alongside, and sometimes across, the road from Littleport to Shippea Hill. The few houses along this road are nearly all built on the rodden, for it provides a firmer foundation than the peat.

The Romans made a road known as Akerman Street across the fens to the higher ground where Ely now stands and this continued at least as far as Littleport. Part of the present road follows the same route in a long straight stretch abreast of Denney Abbey. They also made a canal, named the Car Dyke, which connected the Rivers Cam and Ouse and enabled water-borne traffic to be conveyed from Cambridgeshire to Lincoln and York by means of other connecting waterways. East Anglia was then, as now, a great grain growing district and the canal was used for taking this produce to the garrisons in the north.

By the end of the Roman occupation of Britain, the fen country again became waterlogged and ceased to be settled. When the Angles and Saxons came they chose the higher ground and the margins of the fen for their dwellings, using the fen only for hunting and fishing. The fen assumed the appearance which later influenced the history of Ely. It was a waste of meres and watercourses with islands often rising only a few inches above the water level. Thick beds of reeds grew to more than the height of a man; fish and fowl abounded, providing a living for the half-wild, independent people who dared to settle in the fever-ridden swamps. They alone could find their way with ease in the maze of channels and tracks. Ely became indeed an island for practical purposes.

Although the Anglo-Saxon period lasted for about six hundred years, few remains have been found in the immediate vicinity of Ely, except the late pagan Anglo-Saxon cemetery recently found near the supposed site of Cratendune and weapons of much later date found in rivers, which probably were lost in the course of the fighting with the Normans under William the Conqueror.

The Isle of Ely was situated near the boundary of two of the great Anglo-Saxon kingdoms, East Anglia and Mercia. East Anglia consisted of the present counties of Norfolk and Suffolk and part of Essex, while Mercia covered what are now the Midland counties. The isolated Isle of Ely belonged to a tribe of Britons

known as the Gyrvii.   In the country near Ely people can still be
seen with black hair, round skulls, and a cast of countenance which
reminds us of the Welsh.   These people are perhaps descendants
of the Celtic tribes who, like the Welsh and Cornishmen, successfully resisted the Roman and Saxon invaders.   Until the past
forty years when motor buses have penetrated at least once a
week to most of the fen villages, fenmen have lived secluded lives,
marrying women from their own or neighbouring districts, and
this may have assisted in preserving the purity of the racial strain
in the population.

CHAPTER II

# The Story of St. Etheldreda

In 597 A.D. St. Augustine, a great Roman missionary, came to Kent to try to convert the pagan Saxons to Christianity. He was well received by the King of Kent and people all over the country became enthusiastic supporters of the new religion. Among them was Anna, the King of East Anglia, who lived at Exning, a village close to present-day Newmarket, and only about twelve miles from Ely. The King had four daughters, Etheldreda, Sexburga, Ethelburga and Withburga. It is the story of Etheldreda which concerns us most, though Sexburga and Withburga enter into the history of Ely as well.

Like her father, Etheldreda became an ardent Christian and would like to have devoted her life to religion, but for political reasons it became desirable to marry her to Tonbert, the Prince of the South Gyrvii, whose territory bordered East Anglia. The wedding took place in the year 652 and, as a dowry, Tonbert gave Etheldreda the land and royal rights of the Isle of Ely. Tonbert died three years later leaving Etheldreda a rich young widow but still anxious to pursue the religious life. For five years she lived on her estates, but once again policy necessitated her marriage to a prince, this time Egfrith, heir to the Kingdom of Bernicia in the north of England. Egfrith was much younger than Etheldreda and the marriage was not happy. After twelve years she obtained her husband's consent to retire from worldly affairs and she entered the convent of the Abbess Ebba, King Egfrith's aunt, at Coldingham, where she received the veil and clothing of a nun at the hands of Bishop Wilfrid. A year later she set out for the Isle of Ely. Egfrith pursued Etheldreda, but an inundation of the roads delayed him and she escaped. She had decided to renounce the world and enter a convent, and when she arrived at her estates she looked for a suitable site to build one.

At that time there was no one living where the city of Ely now stands, but there was a village named Cratendune just south of the present road from Ely to Witchford. According to a tradition which cannot be traced back earlier than Norman times, a Christian church had been founded there by Ethelbert in 607, at the instigation of St. Augustine. Etheldreda chose a site about a mile to the north of Cratendune, and there she founded a monastery for both nuns and monks in the year 673. In those days it was easy for

5

anyone to set up a monastic establishment and obtain a charter which granted privileges. The inhabitants of Cratendune abandoned their village and moved to the vicinity of the monastery. Thus it is possible to say exactly when Ely began to exist.

Etheldreda was assisted in her project by Bishop Wilfrid, whom she had met while living in Northumbria. It is from the Venerable Bede, who knew Bishop Wilfrid personally, that we have learned the story of Etheldreda. Bishop Wilfrid consecrated Etheldreda abbess of the monastery, which she continued to rule for some years, setting an example by her piety and disdain for comfort. hot baths were regarded by her as a luxury and she took only about four a year, and those at times of important religious festivals. She became a victim of plague which caused a large swelling in her throat. This was lanced by her surgeon, but she died on 23rd June, 679.

On account of her saintly life, it was decided to remove Etheldreda's remains from the grave where they had been buried to a tomb inside the abbey church. Sixteen years after her death the grave was opened in the presence of Bishop Wilfrid, her sister Sexburga, who had succeeded her as abbess, and several other witnesses. It was alleged that her body was found to be uncorrupted. In order to provide her with a suitable coffin, search had been made for a stone from which one could be made, but a Roman coffin of suitable size was found at Grantchester, near Cambridge. The body was laid in this coffin and taken to a shrine in the church, where it remained for nearly nine hundred years. 17th October, the date of her translation, or second burial, has been observed as her festival until the present day.

Etheldreda's sister Withburga, who had been one of her nuns, founded a nunnery of her own at East Dereham in Norfolk, not many miles away. At her death, Withburga's body was enshrined at Dereham, but in later times the Abbot and monks of Ely wished to have it at their own church with the relics of her sisters. The Abbot Brithnoth gave a feast at Dereham during which monks from Ely came by boat to Brandon and thence by road to Dereham, stole Withburga's body from the church and got it safely away before its loss was discovered. The body was landed at Turbutsea, a spot near the present Beet Sugar Factory, and as late as 1292 there was an entry in the Sacrist's Rolls "Paid for expenses on the feast of St. Withburga the Virgin at Tydbreye, (a variant spelling of Turbutsea) with the brethren and burgesses, 17s. 6d." This would represent as many pounds in our money and shows that the anniversary of the landing of the body of St. Withburga was kept up with considerable enjoyment. The three sisters, together with Eormenilda, daughter of Sexburga, lay in tombs grouped at the east end of the abbey church and attracted many pilgrims.

For some years the life of the monastery went on peacefully, but bad times were coming. The Vikings, Danish pirates from the countries round the Baltic sea, began to invade the country in the same way that the Saxons, who were now settling down fairly peacefully, had done years before. They sailed up the rivers in their light shallow-draught boats, slew the inhabitants, stole their goods, and burnt their buildings, most of which were of wood.

Ely was one of the places which the Vikings burned in this way, and from 870 for a hundred years the monastery lay in ruins while King Alfred and his successors fought the Danes or bribed them to stay away. Finally a settlement was reached and more peaceful times came; the monastery was re-founded by Athelwold, Bishop of Winchester, who obtained permission from King Edgar, and purchased the property which had been the dowry of St. Etheldreda, to endow it. The royal rights were given to the monastery together with rights of two hundreds at Wicklaw in Suffolk, where Woodbridge stands to-day, and the hundred of Mitford in Norfolk. The new monastery at Ely was consecrated in 970 by St. Dunstan and flourished. It received favours from the Danish King of England, Canute, and a poem concerning an incident which occurred during one of his visits to Ely has been handed down to us. It runs as follows:—

> "Merie sungen the Muneches binnen Ely
> Tha Cnut ching rew ther by.
> Rowe ye cnites noer the lant,
> And here we thes Muneches saeng,"

which may be literally translated:

> Merrily sang the monks of Ely
> As Canute the king rowed by.
> Row nearer the land, knights,
> And let us hear these monks sing.

We can believe that the singing was worth hearing, for at this period England was famous among the countries of Europe for the arts. Most of the lighter arts, such as goldsmiths' work, carving, embroidery, etc., were produced in monasteries and there are records of many treasures at Ely, Peterborough and elsewhere.

The peace with the Danes was short-lived for they came again; but Cambridgeshire stood firm against them, and Ely escaped damage. Alderman Brithnoth set out to fight the Danes and met them in battle at Maldon in Essex, but lost his life. According to his wish, his body was brought to Ely for burial and his bones lie to this day in a niche in Bishop West's Chapel at the east end of the present Cathedral.

Aethelflaed, the widow of Alderman Brithnoth, presented the abbey with "a curtain woven and depicted with the deeds of her husband as a memorial of his virtue." It is thought by Mr. E. Maclagan in his book, *The Bayeux Tapestry*, that this curtain was a similar hanging to the famous Bayeux Tapestry which depicts the story of the visit of Harold to Normandy and the battle of Hastings. The Bayeux Tapestry is later, and Bishop Odo, who is thought to have been responsible for having the tapestry made, probably saw the Brithnoth curtain when he was at Ely, and copied the idea.

Those were rough times and Ely became the refuge of men persecuted by their enemies. Men were cruel then, as they are now, and maimed or blinded each other. Sad tales have been passed down to us by the ancient chroniclers and singers of ballads. One ballad, in particular, tells how Alfred, the young son of King Ethelred, was blinded by Earl Godwin's orders, went to Ely for shelter, but died, and was buried in the abbey church.

The Norman Conquest of 1066 was remarkable for its completeness, but the Isle of Ely became what we have come to term a "pocket of resistance." It was then that the natural defences of the Isle became of prime importance, and were exploited by the Saxon leader, Hereward the Wake.

Hereward was the son of Leofric, Earl of Mercia, and his wife Godiva. He had been exiled to the Continent and had lived a very adventurous life. Returning to his estates at Bourne in Lincolnshire in 1068, he found that they had been given to a Norman, Ivo de Taillebois, by William the Conqueror. After a number of adventures, including the sacking of the monastery at Peterborough, which he did to forestall the Norman abbot Turold, he went to Ely and took command of the Saxons who defied the Normans. William was encamped with his army at Brandon, but could not find a way through the fens. Hereward actually penetrated the Norman camp in the disguise of a potter, to spy on his enemies.

Finding that he could not make a successful attack upon Ely from the direction of Brandon, William moved his army to Cambridge, and tried to gain access to the Isle of Ely across causeways at Stuntney, Little Thetford and Aldreth. He was prevented from doing so by Hereward and his followers, and only took Ely in the end through the treachery of the monks, who showed him a route through the fens. In spite of their betrayal of their Saxon defenders, William exacted a heavy penalty from the monks, and the abbot only obtained pardon after making a journey with a number of his monks to Warwick, and the payment of a thousand

THE MARRIAGE OF ST. ETHELDREDA AND EGFRITH

From an engraving in Bentham's *History* of one of the 14th c. carvings in the Octagon.

*Plate 1*

*Plate* 2       WEST FRONT OF THE CATHEDRAL

*oto by*]
WEST TOWER FROM THE COLLEGE

Photo by]							[G. H. Tyndall
Plate 4							THE NAVE, LOOKING EAST

pounds.   It is recorded that in order to satisfy William the monks had to melt down or sell almost all the gold and silver objects in the church, including "crosses, altars, shrines, tissues, chalices, patens, basins, buckets, fistulas, goblets, dishes, and above all the figure of St. Mary with the Child seated on a throne of wonderful workmanship which Abbot Elsin (died 1016) had made"; also four wooden figures of Virgins enriched with gold and silver and precious stones.

Ely was the second richest monastery in England at the time of the Domesday survey made by William I.  According to the calculations of Dom David Knowles in his scholarly book, *The Monastic Order in England*, the gross yearly income of the monastery at that time was £768 17s. 3d.  It must be remembered that the value of a pound was very much greater in those days than it is now; so that this income would have been ample to support the monks and their staff of servants, besides providing for the maintenance of the fabric of the monastic buildings.

Although no trace of the Saxon abbey church remains there is a strong probability that it was built on the Carolingian plan which can still be seen in some churches of that period on the Continent. Originally the church was probably without aisles but it is recorded that Abbot Elsin (981-1016) rebuilt and enlarged the south aisle.   In such buildings the east and west ends were of equal importance and the present arrangement at Ely with a western transept with towers for each is evidently a relic of the old tradition.

CHAPTER III

# The Norman Builders

As soon as the Norman Conquest of England was complete there was a great wave of building activity, which took the form of very large and impressive abbeys and cathedrals. Not many smaller churches were built yet and there are few remains of military or domestic buildings left to-day. Even castles were built of wood, and although the great mounds on which they were built for greater safety still stand, the wood has perished or has been superseded by masonry of a later date. One such castle was built at Ely on the mound known as Cherry Hill, but it did not last for very long. It was used in the wars between King Stephen and Matilda, but evidently not after that period. Looking down towards the east from Cherry Hill one can trace mounds which mark the site of the "bailey" or court-yard of the castle.

Ely, like most of the great abbeys of the Norman period, was what is known as a Benedictine abbey, because the monks lived according to the rule of life set out by St. Benedict. The re-founded monastery, which was in existence before the arrival of the Normans, belonged to the Benedictine rule, and it had a stone abbey church, which stood, so far as we know, slightly to the east and south of the present building. The first church of St. Etheldreda was possibly built of wood, though we cannot be sure. There is still a piece of stone carving of the time of St. Etheldreda in existence in Ely, and it may well be that it formed part of her church. We can see it built into the wall of St. Mary's Barn in St. John's Road, over a blocked up doorway. It shows a man, blowing a horn, with an animal which appears to be an ox. Another relic of the same period stands in the south aisle of the nave of the Cathedral. It is the base and part of a stone cross which was erected to the memory of Ovin, the steward and faithful servant of St. Etheldreda. Ovin managed the estates of Queen Etheldreda in the Isle of Ely and, like her, embraced the monastic life. After his death he was regarded as a saint. We can still read the Latin inscription which asks us to pray for him. The only other Saxon remains which have been found at Ely are some stones which formed part of a window, and they are kept in the Cathedral store with other worked stones from the building. Builders in the past were apt to use stones from old buildings when building new ones, in order to save expense, and many carved stones which must have come from the old monastery are still to be seen in the walls of houses and gardens in various parts of Ely.

Unfortunately we have no record of the size or appearance of the Saxon abbey. It is safe to assume that it was fairly large because it was so important. Modern research has shown that the Saxons were artistic builders using decoration of classical origin which came to them from the ancient city of Byzantium, now named Istambul, in modern Turkey. Byzantium was the eastern capital of the Roman Empire and after the fall of Rome it became the artistic centre of the world. The Saxon craftsmen were clever, and in addition to the tapestry already mentioned there is a record that Abbot Brithnoth had four statues of the Virgin made which were covered with gold, silver, and precious stones, and also a silver crucifix, the body of which was hollowed and contained relics of two saints. These ornaments were made by a local artist named Leo, but they were taken from the abbey at the time of the Conquest. For a time the skill of the Saxon craftsmen was neglected and the cruder Norman work predominated, but a hundred years later the two races united to produce the lovely architecture and stone carving which is so well represented at Ely.

The Norman abbey was begun by Abbot Simeon, brother of Bishop Walkelin of Winchester, who was already building the great cathedral there. Although he was ninety years of age when he came to Ely, Abbot Simeon started to build the abbey in 1083, and continued to inspire the work till his death ten years later. Simeon was one of the great men introduced into England by William I. He was Prior of Winchester before coming to Ely, and won the love and respect of the monks of both monasteries. After the Conquest some of the Saxon monks were moved from one community to another, and some from Winchester followed Simeon to Ely.

The eastern side of the north transept at Ely is the work of Abbot Simeon; the remainder of his work perished when the central tower fell. It will be noticed that the pillars are plainer than the later ones in the nave and that the carving and arches are coloured in some places. When the building was new, the stone was not bare inside as we have been accustomed to see it, but painted with bright colours, at first with designs and later with pictures of well-known stories from the Bible or the lives of the Saints. These pictures have worn away with time in most churches, or have been whitewashed over. Where whitewashing has been done there has been a greater chance of the paintings being preserved, for not only have the colours been protected from the effects of sunlight but also from the notice of the iconoclastic

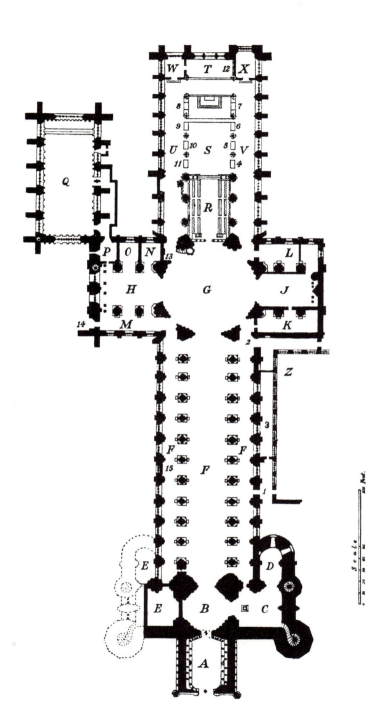

## PLAN OF ELY CATHEDRAL

The plan shows the Cathedral as it was in 1968.

A   West, or Galilee Porch.
B   West Tower.
C   South-west Transept, with Font.
D   St. Catharine's Chapel.
E   Site of North-west Transept and Chapel.
F   Nave and Aisles.
G   Octagon.
H   North-eastern Transept.
J   South-eastern Transept.
K   Clergy Vestry.
L   Library and Chapel of St. Dunstan and St. Ethelwold.
M   Western Aisle of North Transept.
N   St. Edmund's Chapel.
O   Cambridgeshire Regiment War Memorial Chapel.
P   North Porch and entrance to the Lady Chapel.
Q   Lady Chapel.
R   Choir. Choir Stalls on either side.
S   Presbytery, with High Altar.
T   St. Etheldreda's Chapel (County War Memorial).
U   North Choir-aisle, with staircase to the Organ Loft.
V   South Choir-aisle.
W   Bishop Alcock's Chapel, 1500.
X      ,,   West's Chapel, 1534.
Z   Remains of the Cloister.

1   The Prior's Door.
2   The South, or Monks', Door.
3   Choir Vestry.
4   The Tomb of Bishop de Luda, 1298.
5   ,,   ,,   ,,  Bishop Barnett, 1374.
6   ,,   ,,   ,,  John Tiptoft, Earl of Worcester, 1490.
7   ,,   ,,   ,,  Bishop Hotham, 1337.
8   ,,   ,,   ,,  Bishop Northwold, 1254.
9   Remains of the reputed Shrine of St. Etheldreda. Believed to be the super-structure of Bishop Hotham's Tomb.
10   The Tomb of Bishop Kilkenny, 1256.
11   ,,   ,,   ,,  Bishop Redman, 1505.
12   ,,   ,,   ,,  Cardinal Luxemburg, 1443.
13   ,,   ,,   ,,  Dean Caesar, 1635.
14   Wren's Door.
15   The Tomb of Bishop Woodford, 1885.

reformers of the Reformation and Civil War. The remains of a picture of the martyrdom of St. Edmund, King of East Anglia, who was shot to death with arrows by the Danes while he was tied to a tree, can be seen in the chapel dedicated to his memory in the north transept at Ely. The background alone remains, showing the outlines of the figures distinctly.

Other painted decoration is still to be seen on the ceiling of the south aisle close to the South Door. Faint traces of a kind of "barber's pole" design can be seen round the edges of the third and fourth arches from the Octagon on the north side of the nave. This, and the painting in the south aisle, was done in the time of Bishop Ridel (1174-1189), who was alive at the time of the murder of St. Thomas à Beckett, at Canterbury. On some of the pillars in the nave the remains of a very thin coating of plaster can be seen, painted with lines to make it look like stonework. On some of these columns, too, are masons' marks, the plaster still clinging to some of the incisions showing that they have not been scratched by mischievous visitors. These marks are believed to have been made by the stonemasons who cut the stones so that their work could be identified when it was assessed for payment.

At the death of Abbot Simeon the revenue of the monastery was seized by Ralph Flambard, the minister of William Rufus, and no abbot was appointed till the accession of Henry I in 1100, seven years later. The new abbot appointed that year was named Richard. He proceeded with the building of the abbey church, following the plans of Abbot Simeon, and so far completed it that he was able to open the eastern portion and transfer to it the bodies of Saints Etheldreda, Sexburga, Withburga and Eormenilda. Abbot Richard suggested that Ely should be made into a bishopric with the abbey as its cathedral church, but he died before this could be done. His successor, Hervé le Breton became the first Bishop of Ely as well as titular head of the monastery in 1109. A curious reminder of this dual capacity of the bishops of Ely still remains, for there is no bishop's throne at Ely as in other cathedral churches. As abbot, the bishop occupied the stall on the south side of the entrance of the choir and the prior occupied that on the north side. At the time of the dissolution of the monasteries the last prior became the first dean of the newly constituted Cathedral and continued to occupy his old stall, while the bishop retained his stall as titular abbot.

The creation of the bishopric at Ely gave the bishops unusual powers and reduced the wealth and power of the monastery.

At the time when the bishopric was created, Ely showed signs of becoming a large and powerful monastery. The monks owned large estates and with them had inherited the royal prerogatives which had belonged to Queen Etheldreda. In order to provide an income for the bishop the estates were divided, and the monks, probably justly, complained that they got the worst of the bargain. The bishop took to himself the temporal rights and these were not finally taken away from his successors till 1836. The bishop nominated the chief justice for the Isle of Ely, who could hear all criminal and civil pleas in the island. Cases could be transferred from the King's courts at Westminster to the bishop's court at Ely, and this proved to be a convenience for local people who wished to plead.

For some years after this change the importance of Ely as a monastery was small. Bishop Hervé expressly absolved himself and his successors from any responsibility for the fabric of the cathedral, though later bishops were often most generous in their contributions towards building projects. The division of the wealth and power of the monastery was probably welcome to the King, who feared that the combination of them with the natural defences of the Isle might be of danger in the event of a rebellion. The number of monks at the monastery in 1110 was about fifty, but at a later date it had increased to seventy-two, with a similar number of servants. In the time of William I the monastery had to support forty knights, and it was possibly that number who lived at the monastery with the monks for a time, after the Isle had been finally conquered by the Normans.

There is no record of any building at the cathedral during the time of Bishop Hervé. The Bishop was busy arranging the business affairs of the new see, and made a journey to Rome for the Pope's approval. A stormy period followed. The next bishop was Nigel (1133-1169), and there is no record of any work being done to the building during his time at Ely. Bishop Nigel was involved in the troubles of King Stephen's reign. He first supported Stephen, but later changed sides and joined Matilda. Bishop Nigel built the castle at Ely which has already been mentioned. His followers were attacked by King Stephen's men and sent to Geoffrey de Mandeville for help. Geoffrey came to the Isle, but it was blockaded by the King's troops and the monks had the doubtful pleasure of seeing their defenders use up the produce of the Isle while their property elsewhere was being ravaged by the King's troops. Much of their treasure had to be sold for food and more of it had been taken by Bishop Nigel who had gone to Rome.

It is recorded that Bishop Ridel, who followed Nigel in 1174, built the western end of the Cathedral, so we may conclude that by the end of his episcopate in 1189 the building was substantially complete.   With the exception of the east end, most of it survives to-day.   The completed building consisted of the nave, as we know it, the eastern transepts, and beyond them four bays and an apse which have been removed.   From the foundations, the apse was evidently first intended to be round but it was made square.   It was removed when Bishop Northwold's presbytery was built in 1235, and the four bays of the Norman choir were destroyed when the short, square Norman tower fell in 1323.   At the western end of the building was the tall tower, which was about sixty feet shorter than it is to-day.   The single great tower at the west end was a Saxon tradition which survived at Ely, whereas most other great churches of the period have two towers at the west end, or one in the middle.   Ely had western transepts, only one of which survives. It is easy to imagine how fine the west front must have appeared when they were both standing.   It had taken a century to complete the building which has now stood in its completeness for nearly eight hundred years.

Inside the building the effect of the great nave is magnificent and almost takes one's breath away when first seen.   The huge pillars support three tiers of arches to a great height;  but the eye is also carried forward by them to the dim distance beyond the brightly lit nave.   For variety, the pillars are of two main types arranged alternately.   If we examine them closely we shall see a slight refinement of workmanship creeping in as they approach the west end, and in the west tower and transept there are details suggesting the transition from the round-arched Norman style to the pointed arch of the Early English style of architecture which followed.   Referring to the nave, Mr. E. S. Prior, in his book *Eight Chapters on Medieval Art*, says "The setting out of the piers can be seen to propose a great achievement of masonry in the throwing of arches over the wide nave at some eighty feet from the floor level.   Though in this case not carried out, the disposition is that of an ordered scheme, conceived in the masonic forethought of master builders."

A prominent feature of the interior of the nave for six hundred years was the stone pulpitum, or screen, which divided the nave into two portions and impeded the vista which is one of the great features of the cathedral to-day.   It was in the form of a solid wall pierced by three door-ways and was decorated with arcading.

Outside the building the appearance has been altered by the insertion of windows at different times, but if we want to see what it looked like when it was new, there is still one portion of the building in its original state on the east side of the north transept, between the Choir and the Lady Chapel.   Here the exterior of the

*Plate* 5 THE CHOIR, LOOKING WEST

two upper storeys and the parapet of the roof remain as they were in Norman times, but the windows of the bottom storey have been altered at a later period.   Reference to the south aisle of the nave will show us what the lower windows were like when first built.

CHAPTER IV

# The Monastery Buildings

WHILE the Cathedral was being built the monks were not neglecting the very necessary living accommodation for a large community such as theirs. There was a conventional plan for a Benedictine monastery which was always followed where the site would permit. Ely is typical. On the south side of the nave of the abbey church was the cloister, a large square plot of ground surrounded by a covered walk in which the monks carried out their studies and various kinds of work. To the south of the cloister was the refectory, or dining hall, beyond which was the kitchen which served it on one side, and the great hall where visitors were entertained, on the other. Very little remains of the cloister at Ely and still less of the refectory, but for many years the great hall served as the Deanery until it became the Bishop's House in 1941. In the garden may be seen some of the great Norman columns which formed part of the kitchen. Still further to the south, and almost adjoining the great hall, were the Prior's House and other buildings for the entertainment of visitors to the monastery; for in the Middle Ages it did duty as a kind of hotel where people could stay for a night or two without question or charge.

The space immediately to the south of the south transept of the abbey church was the site of the Chapter House, where the monks met to discuss matters concerning the government and business of the establishment. The Dorter, or Dormitory, formed the upper storey of a building which occupied the space taken up by the present roadway along the east side of the cloister. The positions of all these buildings can be seen in the plan on pages 24 and 25.

To the east of these buildings was the Infirmary where the sick or aged monks lived. We can still see the nave of the building. The roof has gone and the aisles have been converted into houses in more recent times. At the end of the infirmary is the chapel which belonged to it. It too is open to the sky and the chancel has become a room in one of the houses. These houses are occupied by the Dean, Canons and Minor Canons of the Cathedral.

Other buildings which housed the Sacrist and the Almoner stood away from the Cathedral on the north side, backing onto the High Street. The Sacrist was responsible for the services at the altar and for the upkeep of the building and its furnishings. When

18

building work was going on, the workshops of the craftsmen were located near the Sacristy, as his house was called. The almoner was responsible for giving alms and food to the poor who came daily to the monastery. There was a gateway beyond his house opening into the Market Place, and it was to this that the poor came for the surplus food from the monastic table. They were also given the cast-off clothing of the monks who purposely gave away their garments before they were badly worn so that they should be more serviceable to the poor.

In the Middle Ages what are now known as "Social Services" were all carried on by the monasteries. Education was provided free and the present Kings' School and Choir School at Ely are the successors of schools founded by the monks. The Kings' School claims a record going back for a thousand years. King Edward the Confessor was presented at the altar of the abbey in infancy and as a child was educated in the cloister school, with the singing, or choir, boys.

Monks were expected to live like gentlemen and a list of clothes which they had to have was very costly. Each monk brought his own bedding with him when he first came to the monastery; the list of linen shows that there was a fair degree of comfort. Mattresses were filled with straw which was changed once a year. Clothing and linen were renewed annually.

The science of medicine was not very far advanced in the Middle Ages, but such as it was was administered by the monks. One of the buildings adjoining the Infirmary was known as the Blood-letting House because it was there that the monks were "bled." Once every seven weeks each of the monks underwent this operation, for it was considered good for their health to have surplus blood removed. Blood donors of the present day find that there are no ill effects from the loss of a pint of blood, but the practice of blood letting has died out during the past century. The monks probably enjoyed the experience, for not only were their duties reduced for a few days but they enjoyed the better food which was provided to restore their strength. There is a record that for the week beginning on the 1st August, 1388, the provision for seven monks who had been "bled" and eleven other patients in the Infirmary, included beef, mutton, pork, veal, pullets, capons, salt and fresh fish, eggs, milk, cream, mustard, cheese, and spices. Medicines were compounded largely of spices, some of which are used only as flavourings in cooking nowadays. Ginger figures largely in the accounts of the Infirmary.

In addition to providing medical services, the monks were patrons and exponents of the arts of painting, sculpture, architecture, goldsmith's work, and other crafts. They copied manuscripts in beautiful script with delicate illustrations in gold and brilliant colours which are as fresh to-day as when they were first done.

The monks, as we have seen, owned large estates which needed managing or farming. They built roads or bridges where necessary for better communication between different parts of their property. The present road from Ely to Stuntney and Soham is built on a causeway made by the monks across the fen, and the original Ely High Bridge was built by them too. The produce from the farms was brought to the large barn just inside the monastery gate. Fish, an important item of the monastic diet, were kept in ponds in the park, and the depressions in the ground where these ponds used to be can still be seen. A road in Ely, named "The Vineyards," commemorates the fact that the bishop and the monks grew grapes for wine, though it is thought that it was of poor quality and used as vinegar. Good wine for the table was imported from France. Beer was the popular drink for the monks and several varieties were brewed in the monastery.

The property of the monks caused a good deal of legal work, and much of the information which has been handed down to us has been in the form of deeds. The monks had a filing system. Each document bore certain letters and numbers which corresponded with those on compartments in long narrow boxes in which the parchments were kept. Some of these boxes are still preserved in the Cathedral library. The labels are written in red and black on slips of parchment and give a list of the documents housed in each compartment.

It is interesting to note that the earlier documents, for instance those of the Norman period, are more legible than later ones. Evidently as writing became a more common accomplishment less care was taken over it, and the shapes of letters became debased. The 18th and 19th centuries brought a revival of fine writing, but the present-day craze for speed and the fact that writing is not a special subject in schools, have combined to produce the present poor standard. The saving of time only benefits the writer, for the reader wastes much time in deciphering it.

The daily life of a monk was based upon an entirely different system from that of any walk of life in the western world to-day. He rose at midnight or two o'clock in the morning and went to bed correspondingly early. It was about ten hours before his first meal. Most of the day was taken up by a series of services in church and the intervals were filled by the duties allotted to him. He had few meals, which were further curtailed during periods of fasting. The food was plentiful but not popular, for it is recorded that a strict watch had to be kept to make sure that the monks did not eat elsewhere than in the refectory.

Because of their superior learning, abbots and bishops rose to the most responsible positions in the state. Ely, in particular, provided several chancellors for the kings of the Middle Ages. Business took the bishops of Ely to London so frequently that they had a palace at Holborn, and subsequently a house in Dover Street which they retained until about 1900. It has recently become the offices of Oxford University Press. The house was built in 1772-6.

The bishops of those days had palaces at several places in their diocese but it was not till the end of the fifteenth century that the present Palace at Ely was commenced by Bishop Alcock. Some remains of the Palace at Little Downham, three miles away, may still be seen. At one time it stood in a deer park, but the existing portion of the building has been turned into a farmhouse and is surrounded by fields.

Like most princes, bishops maintained large households which went from place to place exhausting the hospitality of each in turn. A visit from a bishop or king was a financial disaster for even the wealthiest. Roads were bad, and the account rolls of the monastery reveal constant expense for materials to keep them in repair. Travel by water was the most satisfactory form and was the common mode of transport in the Fenland. It was by water that the stones and timber for the building of the Cathedral were transported to Ely, and we read of Turbutsea, now the site of the Beet Sugar Factory, as being the landing place.

## CHAPTER V

# The Medieval Builders

ALTHOUGH the Normans left a complete Cathedral at Ely it was not long before the monks began to make additions to it, and later, alterations which were found to be necessary as a result of changing conditions and needs. The first of these building works was the west, or Galilee Porch. One explanation of the term "Galilee" is that in the course of the Sunday procession a "station" was made there and the cantor sang, "Behold I go before you into Galilee." There are several other explanations in circulation.

The date of the building of the Galilee is disputed, but it was probably about 1200-15, or roughly about the time when Magna Carta was signed by King John. It is regarded as a very fine example of the Early English style of architecture. In size it is as large as a small church, being forty-two feet long from the outer to the inner door. It has two storeys, though the roof was removed from the upper one in the 18th century. The outside is divided into panels by arcading and inside there is very beautiful arcading in Purbeck marble which has, unfortunately, suffered from the effects of seven hundred years of weather. This was restored 1967-8.

On one of the inside walls of the Galilee there is a graffito, or drawing scratched on the stone, which is obviously one of the mason's working drawings for the west front of the porch. It shows the centre gable rising to a point and a difference in the tracery over the entrance, the alterations which we see now date from the 18th century. There is no doubt that the drawing was made while the work was being done, for a "consecration" cross cuts through part of it and this would have been made when the work was completed. The style of work, and some of the stone, indicate that it was done by masons from Lincoln.

It may be as well, at this point, to explain the difference between the styles of architecture which were in use in England in the Middle Ages. They are broadly classified as Norman or Romanesque, Early English, Decorated and Perpendicular, with transitional periods between them. They are to be found in all parts of the country and conform to period with a little overlapping due to the difference in distance from the source of origin. The uniformity of detail over the whole country may cause surprise in these days when no real style has been developed, and after decades

22

when there was a good deal of imitation of earlier styles. It was
probably due to the influence of the guild system which flourished
in the Middle Ages. The guilds were the predecessors of trade
associations, trade unions, friendly societies, and technical schools,
and were at the same time religious in background. They settled
terms of apprenticeship, protected their members and laid down
standards. In the case of stone masons the element of Freemasonry,
which has now become divorced from the trade, entered into the
lives of the members. Opposite St. Mary's Church is a house which
is believed to have once been a guild hall. In many parish churches
in large towns there are side chapels which were built at the expense
of local guilds and which they used for their services and for
masses for departed members.

The Norman style of architecture is typified at Ely by the remains
of the building as described in Chapter III. The term "Romanesque" covers not only the Norman style, which was common in
England during the 12th century, but buildings all over western
Europe built during the period. The name is derived from the
fact that Roman methods were copied. The construction was
massive; arches, vaults and windows were round. There was
little carved decoration, though at the end of the period what there
was was often very elaborate in design. The outside of the
Prior's Door at Ely is an outstanding example of late Norman
carving. The door led from the south aisle of the nave into the
Cloister and with the South Door, sometimes known as the Monks'
Door, formed an entrance and exit for ceremonial processions.
The South Door is not so fine as the Prior's Door. It dates from

## PLAN OF THE MONASTERY AT ELY

THE plan on the following page shows the arrangement of the
monastic buildings as they were shortly before the dissolution in
the time of Henry VIII. The general arrangement was the same
for the four hundred years from the beginning of the 12th century,
when the earliest existing buildings were begun; but many additions
and alterations were made from time to time to provide for changing
conditions. The walls shown in solid black in the plan are still
standing. They form part of buildings which house the Bishop,
Dean and Canons, and the Kings' School. Walls shown as dotted
lines are non-existent but either foundations have been discovered
or their previous existence is presumed from other evidence.
The plan is adapted from one made by Mr. S. Inskip Ladds,
F.R.I.B.A., with his kind permission. Mr. Ladds' fuller plan
appears in his book *The Monastery of Ely*, which was reprinted from
the Transactions of the Cambs. & Hunts. Archaeological Society.

# Plan of the Monastery

A  The Cloister.
B  Site of the Chapter House.
C  „  „  Refectory, or Dining Hall.
D  Site of the Parlour and entrance to the Cloister.
E  Site of the Dorter, or Dormitory.
F  „  „  Monks' Kitchen.
G  The Great Hall, or Guest Hall.
H  Site of the Prior's Kitchen.
I  The Fair Hall, or Queen's Hall.
J  The Prior's House.
K  Site of Prior Crauden's Study.
L  Porch, with King's Treasury above.
M  Prior Crauden's Chapel.
N  Site of the Bake-house.
O  Accommodation for visitors.
P  Malt-house.
Q  Ely Porta: the great gate-house of the Monastery.
R  Stables.

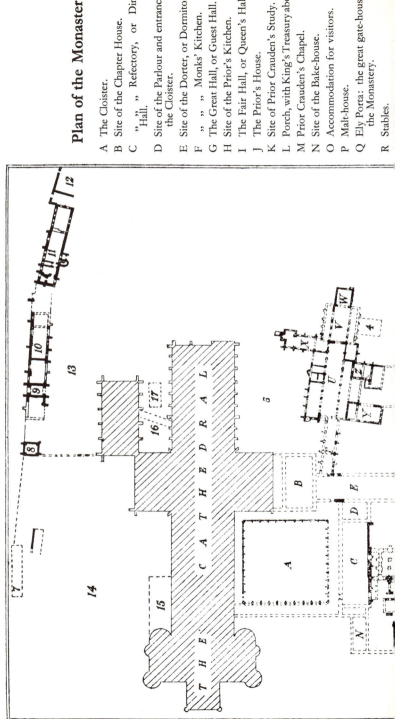

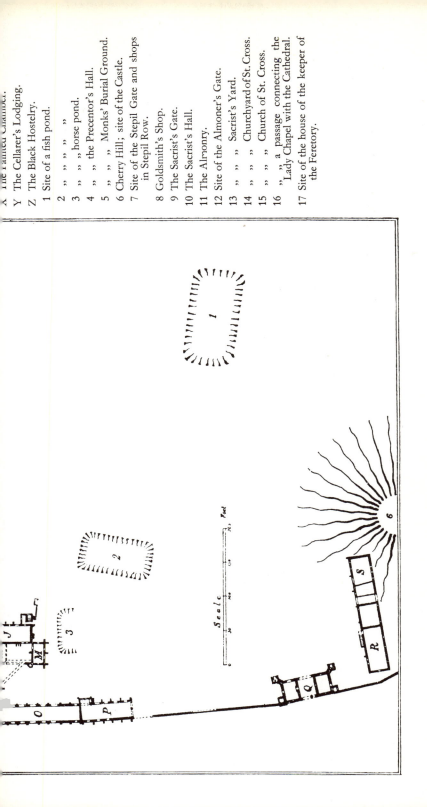

about the year 1150, the Prior's Door being about twenty years
later.    The style of carving shows that at that period sculptors had
not yet mastered the technique of carving in the round and were
trying to make copies of drawings.    The style of the Prior's Door
is that of what is known as the Winchester School of drawing,
particularly in respect of the drapery.    There is a good deal of
distortion about the figures but the whole work repays careful
examination.

The chief examples of the Early English style at Ely are the
Galilee Porch, which has already been described, and the Presbytery.
The newer style of architecture is lighter in character than that
of the Normans.    The science of building was better understood
in the 13th century, which was roughly the period during which
Early English architecture flourished.    Stresses and thrusts were
allowed for, and vaulting, instead of being solid or divided by plain
intersecting arches, was built up with ribs of stone locked by key
stones at the intersections, the intervening spaces being filled with
a thin web of stone.    The key stones, or bosses as they are called,
provided good oportunities for stone carvers to make lovely
designs in foliage, faces, or scenes from the Bible and these are
usually gilded and brightly coloured.    If we look up at the roofs
of the Presbytery, Choir and Lady Chapel at Ely we can see good
examples of this type of decoration.

Early English windows were larger than those of the Norman
period, partly because stained glass was coming into fashion.
Very often the earlier windows had no glass at all and shutters were
used to keep out the weather.    The tops of Early English and
later styles of windows were usually pointed.    The earliest type
was a single pointed opening called a lancet, but soon two, three,
five or more lancets were grouped together, as in the case of the
east window at Ely.    Notice that although there are only two tiers
of lancets visible from the inside there are three to be seen from
outside.    The topmost tier of lancets lights the space between the
top of the vault and the high-pitched timber roof.    Later in the
period the builders became more venturesome and reduced the
amount of stonework between the lancets so much that the whole
merged into one window.    The odd spaces at the top were pierced
with holes of different designs.    This was the beginning of tracery,
and is known as plate tracery.    The later form was a design made
out of thin curved bars of stone instead of holes being cut through
blocks.    Finally in a still later period vast areas of glass were
supported by a minimum of mullions and tracery.    An example
can be seen in the Lady Chapel at Ely which belongs to the
Decorated period of architecture.

Instead of massive pillars we find clusters of delicate shafts, often of Purbeck marble, which was transported from Dorset by sea. There is much more carved decoration particularly in the form of foliage, which, during a short period, was an exact copy of nature. Figure sculpture reached a very high level, particularly in the case of effigies on tombs. Early English stone carving was deeply cut in order to give a greater effect of light and shade.

All these features are to be seen in the beautiful Presbytery at Ely. This is the name given to the six easternmost bays of the building which were added by Bishop Hugh de Northwold, mainly at his own expense. The work cost £5,350 18s. 8d., a sum which probably represents more than £500,000 of our present-day money. The work was begun in 1235, and was finished and dedicated in the presence of King Henry III and his son Prince Edward on 17th September, 1253. This extension was built mainly to provide a more worthy setting for the tombs of St. Etheldreda and her sisters, which had been placed at the east end of the Norman church. The apse of the old building was removed by Bishop Northwold, but part of the two Norman columns immediately adjoining his work can still be seen. Large numbers of pilgrims visited the shrine in the hope of being cured of their ills and their gifts helped to enrich the monastery. Access was gained through a door near Bishop Alcock's Chapel in the north choir aisle and later another doorway, still to be seen, though disused, was made behind the present site of the organ so that the pilgrims after visiting the shrine could make their way to the Lady Chapel.

Instead of building the Presbytery in the proportions customary at the time, the builders maintained the lines of the Norman building and their example was followed by the designer of the three bays of the Choir which were rebuilt a hundred years later during the first half of the 14th century. It is due to this fact that Ely Cathedral gives such an impression of unity in spite of the variety of styles of architecture to be found in it. Each successive addition to the building was made in the style which was "Modern Architecture" to the men who built it, but their regard for what had gone before and the maintenance of the horizontal lines in the composition have resulted in a pleasing and harmonious whole.

In Godwin's *Catalogue of the Bishops* the following remarks are made about Bishop Northwold: "This man is much commended for his house keeping and liberality unto the poore, which may well seeme strange, considering the infinite deale of money spent by him in building of his church and houses." He died on 6th August, 1254, and was buried under a very fine tomb in the Presbytery which he had built.

# CHAPTER VI

# The Building of St. Mary's Church

DURING the period covered by the previous chapter, other building works were going on at Ely, apart from the Cathedral. Bishop Eustace, who held the see from 1197 till 1215, is known to have rebuilt St. Mary's Church, which stands a few hundred yards to the west of the Cathedral. This is the only indication that there was a previous church on the site, so it is impossible to guess at the date or appearance of the earlier church. The present church suffers from being so close to such an important building as the Cathedral; if it were the chief church of the town it would receive more attention from visitors and no doubt it would contain more monuments of interest. However, anyone who takes the trouble to examine the building will find it a good example of its period.

The principal entrance is now by the north door, which displays all the usual features of late Norman or Transitional work. It is thought that the south door was originally the principal entrance, as more houses lay on that side of the church in early times. The chief features of the interior are the columns, which are taller and more slender than the earlier Norman style, though still plain and round. They support pointed arches, with very little decoration, and stand on rough square bases. From their appearance it has been thought that at some time the level of the floor has been lowered in order to give an effect of greater height to the interior of the building.

The church consists of a nave with aisles, a side chapel on the south side, a chancel at a higher level, tower with spire, and a modern vestry. The chancel has lancet windows at the sides and an east window of a later date. The proportions of this window are not pleasing as they give the effect of its being the upper part of a taller one. It is filled with modern stained glass depicting the adoration of the shepherds.

The tower and spire are of the Decorated period, later than the remainder of the church. There is a peal of eight bells which were re-hung in 1939. In the following year, the side chapel, which for many years had been filled with pews facing the body of the church, was cleared, re-furnished, and restored to its original use. In the east wall of this chapel there is a modern stained-glass window showing scenes connected with the history of Ely and including a view of the Cathedral.

In different parts of the building there are a number of memorial tablets bearing the names of well-known Ely families, but they are of comparatively recent date, belonging mostly to the 18th and 19th centuries.

Outside the church is one of the best kept churchyards in the district, surrounded by old houses, mostly of the timber framed type and probably three or four hundred years old. Reference to old pictures will show, however, that some of them have changed in appearance in recent years, becoming more picturesque in the process. In the churchyard, to the south of the church, are the remains of an old Norman font, and a small stone coffin. The font bears an inscription in Latin to the effect that in future it shall receive only the water from Heaven.

On the south wall of the tower is a tablet recording the names of five men who were executed for robbery during the Littleport Riots, a little more than a century ago.

In monastic times St. Mary's Church, and the other churches and religious houses in the city, came under the jurisdiction of the Sacrist of the Monastery. He was the rector and was responsible for the curates who actually conducted the services. Since the Reformation, St. Mary's Church has been served by a vicar who is nominated by the Dean and Chapter of Ely, the successors to the Abbot and monks. Until recently there were two parishes in Ely: Holy Trinity, which had the Lady Chapel of the Cathedral as its parish church, and St. Mary's. Early in this century the two parishes were given into the charge of one vicar, and in 1938 they were united into one benefice and the Lady Chapel handed back to the Dean and Chapter of the Cathedral.

The origin of the use of the Lady Chapel as a parish church is curious. From very early times the nave of the cathedral served as the church of one of the parishes of Ely, but the arrangement was not very satisfactory. In 1315, during the reign of Edward the Second, the monks were ordered by the Archbishop to build a separate church for the parishioners, but did not do so till after 1362, when they built a lean-to building against the outside of the wall of the north aisle of the nave. This church was known as St. Cross, and continued to be used until 1566, when it was pulled down because the parishioners complained that it was "dark and noysome for lack of thurrowe air." It was then that they were given the use of the Lady Chapel to take its place.

Some other Ely buildings, which date from the 13th century, are situated about a quarter of a mile to the west of St. Mary's Church. They are the remains of two small religious houses or hospitals, as they were called. They are at present known as

St. John's Farm and St. Mary's Barn. Both stand at the bottom of St. John's Road, which used to be the main road from Cambridge and Witchford. St. Mary's Barn is a plain building with pointed arches and looks as if it might once have been a chapel. As has already been mentioned in a previous chapter, there is a carved stone of Saxon workmanship, built into the wall over a blocked-up doorway, which, from its design, is judged by experts to date from the end of the 7th century, or roughly from the time of St. Etheldreda.

The chief building of St. John's Farm, which was the larger of these two religious houses, presents a picturesque appearance with its crow-step gables. Close examination has led to the belief that it is part of the nave of a church, the aisles having been removed and the spaces between the pillars filled with masonry. The alterations may have been made when the establishment was dissolved and converted to lay purposes in 1561. It is interesting to note that St. John's Barn is oriented on the same line as St. Mary's Church, and St. Mary's Hospital on the same line as the Cathedral. Most churches are built approximately east and west with the altar at the east end, but there are exceptions and in the case of Ely Cathedral the direction is a good deal south of east. This may be due to a custom which arose of making the "east" window face the rising sun on the feast of the patron saint; but there is no proof of this.

A hospital at Ely is mentioned in 1109, and in 1240 Bishop Northwold amalgamated the two hospitals and put them under the jurisdiction of the Sacrist of the Monastery. The combined establishment escaped the dissolution of the smaller monasteries until 1561, when it was given to Clare College, Cambridge, who continued to own the property until quite recently.

It was during the 13th century that Ely once again became the haven of those who went in fear of their lives. Many of the barons came here who could not pay the fines demanded to recover their estates after the Barons' War of 1264-1265, led by Simon de Montfort against Henry III, and were not finally dislodged till 1267. The approaches to Ely were still few and difficult, just as they had been in the time of Hereward, and the monks had neglected to keep them in repair, probably as a protection against attack during the troubles.

Another event of importance during the 13th century was the founding of Peterhouse, Cambridge, by Bishop Hugh de Balsham in the year 1280. This was the first of the Cambridge colleges; the first Oxford college, Merton, was founded six years previously, thus making Oxford the senior university. The link between the

Cathedral and the University has been maintained to the present day.  The Ely Professor of Divinity at the University is also, by virtue of his office, a Canon of the Cathedral, as was the Regius Professor of Hebrew followed by the Regius Professor of Divinity until about 1940.  Another Cambridge college, namely Jesus College, owes its foundation to Bishop Alcock, who suppressed the Nunnery of St. Radegund and converted it into a college in 1496 in the reign of Henry VII.  Bishops and Deans of Ely have often been great scholars.  For the past two hundred and fifty years it has been an unwritten law that the Bishop should be a member of Cambridge University.

# CHAPTER VII

# The Age of Craftsmen

THE 13th century saw the birth of a distinctive English culture. The Saxons had borrowed from the Greeks. The Normans continued with the Roman building tradition, and with their French ways and language temporarily submerged the native individuality. Later, the wars in the time of King Stephen made life too insecure for cultural development. When the foolish policy of King John lost France and threw the English back on their own resources, sufficient time had elapsed since the Conquest for the two races to intermingle and evolve an architectural style of their own.

By the time the 14th century was reached there was a revival of the arts for, although the Hundred Years' War was proceeding in France, there was comparative peace at home. It was a time when Europe was waking up after the Dark Ages and the first flush of the Renaissance was producing artists and authors in Italy. In those days all people were of one mind about religion. Europe was less nationalistic than she ever has been since, and the scholar could wander where he would and meet kindred spirits. All clerks, as scholars and clerics were called, understood Latin, and so Europe enjoyed a common language, which benefit has only recently been lost, for people of learning used it until the 18th century.

Owing to the peaceful conditions in England unfortified private houses began to be built and church building increased. The style of architecture which developed during this period is known as Decorated from the fact that much carved ornament was used. Window tracery became more elaborate and there was a good deal of stained glass and carved wooden furniture. Goldsmiths were common. There was a family of hereditary goldsmiths at Ely named Salamon, and it is thought that Alan of Walsingham, who figures largely in the history of the Monastery, was a member of this family.

In 1321 the monks of Ely decided to build a Lady Chapel. The cult of the Blessed Virgin had become very popular, and chapels to her honour were being added to most cathedrals and, in some cases, to parish churches as well. The most usual position for the Lady Chapel was at the east end of the existing building, with an entrance contrived beneath the east window; but at Ely the Cathedral was already of so great a length that such an extension would have been inconvenient, as it would have made intercourse

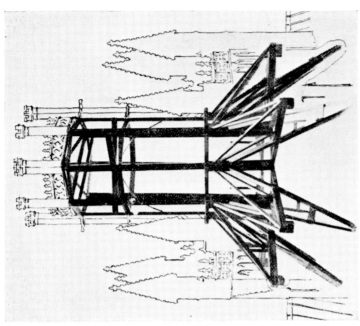

[G. H. Tyndall

Plate 7b    THE FRAMEWORK OF THE LANTERN

Photos by]

Plate 7a    THE LANTERN AND OCTAGON FROM
THE WEST TOWER

Photo by]

[G. H. Tyndall

THE PRIOR'S HOUSE

Plate 8

INTERIOR OF PRIOR CRAUDEN'S CHAPEL

*Plate* 9

*Plate* 10        REMAINS OF THE MONASTIC INFIRMARY

*Plate* 11        THE SACRIST'S GATE

between the portions of the monastery lying to the north and south of the Cathedral difficult, and besides this the monks' burial ground lay on the site. It was decided to build the chapel as a separate building lying to the north of the choir and attached to one corner of the north transept. Access is now gained through the transept, but originally there was a passage leading from a now disused door in the north choir aisle behind the organ.

The Lady Chapel was planned on magnificent lines; much larger than most, the size externally being more than 100 feet by 50, and in an advanced style for the period. All superfluous wall space was dispensed with so that the windows could be as large as possible, but in spite of this there is an exceptionally wide stone vaulted ceiling carried on large buttresses. Round the interior runs an arcade with elaborate carvings depicting the legends of the life of the Virgin, but the iconoclasts of the time of the Reformation defaced them so thoroughly that of the hundreds of figures only one retains its head. Mr. E. S. Prior in his book *Eight Chapters on English Medieval Art*, draws attention to the fact that the sculpture is no longer figure sculpture but a kind of large-scale engraving. He says, "It is not the imager, but the entailer (intagliator) who at Ely tells the story of the Virgin. His interest in the matter is its decorative combination with the bulging canopy-work." The sea-weed-like appearance of the foliage which is a characteristic of this period is noticeable.

With the exception of a few fragments, all the stained glass was destroyed by reformers and in consequence the lighting of the building is too bright. Here and there we can see how the carved stonework was painted in bright colours and outlines in niches show where statues once stood. The roof bosses were too high up for the reformers to reach, so they remained undamaged. There are 123 of them, some depicting Adam and Eve, the Blessed Virgin, and decorative foliage; others are grotesque faces with foliage coming out of their mouths. One is of the head of a negro and is so realistic that it is obvious that it was either done from life or by someone who had seen a negro. This is rather surprising, considering the date.

The building of the Lady Chapel was under the direction of a monk named John de Wisbech, who died during the Black Death which raged in England during 1348-9, killing one-third of the population of the country. The first stone was laid by Alan of Walsingham, the Sacrist, and the building took twenty-eight years and thirteen weeks to complete. There is a legend that the money for the building was provided from a hoard discovered by John de Wisbech while he was digging on the site.

The length of time taken to complete the Lady Chapel was partly due to a catastrophe which occurred the year after it was commenced. In 1322 the square central Norman tower of the Cathedral collapsed, destroying the adjoining bays of the choir. Alan of Walsingham, as Sacrist of the monastery, was responsible for the maintenance of the fabric. He, by a stroke of genius, resolved to rebuild the tower in the hitherto unused form of an octagonal space surmounted by a dome-shaped roof. This was done by removing the remains of the four pillars which had supported the tower and linking the columns of the next bays in choir, transepts, and nave by means of arches set at an angle of 45 degrees. The result is most impressive; four lofty arches are alternated by smaller ones and above these are large windows. The whole is roofed with a wooden vault from the middle of which rises an octagonal wooden lantern tower over sixty feet high.

The stonework of the Octagon took six years to build, but the wood-work of the Lantern took another fourteen years to complete. Difficulty was experienced in finding oak trees large enough to form the main timbers, which are sixty-eight feet in length. How these huge beams were placed in position is a mystery, for although the account rolls for a great part of the period during which the work was going on have been preserved, and we can read of the payments for labour and materials, there is no record of the method of building. The work was done under the direction of a master carpenter named Master William Hurley. He probably designed the structure and devised the means of raising the beams to their present position. The diagram in Plate 7 (*b*) shows the skeleton of the Lantern as it would appear if the casing could be removed. Hurley afterwards became the King's head carpenter in the 14th century equivalent of the Office of Works. The whole of the outside of the Lantern is cased with lead, and when it was new a peal of bells hung in the top storey. Mr. Browne Willis in his *Survey of Ely Cathedral* in 1729 says that Alan of Walsingham employed John de Gloucester, a bell-founder, to cast these bells in the Western Tower or Steeple, viz., the *Mary*, weighing 2180 *l.*; the *John*, 2704 *l.*; the *Jesus*, 3792 *l.*; and the *Walsingham*, 6280 *l.* In *Church Bells of Cambridgeshire* J. J. Raven gives the name of the bell-founder as Henry Penn of Peterborough. These bells were removed from the Lantern by Dean Wilford between 1662 and 1667 and recast to make smaller bells for the West Tower.

Alan of Walsingham enjoyed the friendship and encouragement of two great colleagues in Bishop John de Hotham and Prior John Crauden, whom he eventually succeeded. Bishop Hotham made himself responsible for the cost of rebuilding the three bays of the choir which had been destroyed by the fall of the tower, and which fill the space between the Octagon and Bishop North-wold's presbytery.   Prior Crauden was treated as a personal friend by Queen Phillipa, the Queen of Edward III, and she visited the monastery at different times during the building, being lodged in a building known as the Queen's Hall.   The Octagon was dedicated in the presence of the King and Queen, whose heads may be seen in stone at the base of the hood mould of the arch on the north-east side of the Octagon.   In similar positions on the other arches are portrait sculptures of Bishop Hotham, Prior Crauden, Alan of Walsingham and the Master Mason.   Another series of carvings on the bases of niches on the main piers, depict incidents in the life of St. Etheldreda.

The choir stalls were made at the same time as the Octagon and originally were placed in it, but have been moved twice since. The delicate carving of the canopies is well preserved and the miserere seats depict humorous as well as scriptural scenes.   They are well worth examining.   Fifty-nine of them are original.   They remind us that religion and everyday life were very close to each other in those days, when religion was a joyful thing not reserved for Sundays only.   From these carvings we can see the sort of clothes people wore in the 14th century and what some of the things they used looked like.   Miss M. D. Anderson, who has made a study of the origins of medieval carvings suggests that in many cases they are derived from the "mystery" plays of the time. The miserere which shows the scene where Salome is dancing before Herod was probably based on a stage production; and the carving of Adam and Eve with the Serpent shows how a human actor represented the Serpent by hiding behind some foliage while a dummy tail was entwined round a stem.   All the figures are dressed in the costume of the period when the carving was made.

It has been popularly supposed that work of this type was actually done by the monks themselves, but although there must have been monks who were skilled in carving, or masonry, the records show that most of the work was done by professional builders who were employed by them.   In Norman times a great deal of unskilled labour could be used, but later styles of building demanded precision only to be acquired by long experience.   From the accounts, it can be gathered that the King's master mason was employed in the early stages of the building of the Octagon, but, as time went on, a local mason named John Attegrene took his place.   Attegrene, or atte Grene as he is often called, was later called to London to fill the post of one of the King's chief masons

who died of the Black Death.    Painters and wood carvers employed
at Ely are mentioned by name in the accounts, and apparently they
came from villages in the neighbourhood.    If village craftsmen
could do such fine work in those days surely their descendents
might do the same if they received the necessary encouragement!

While the Lady Chapel and the Octagon were being built, other
work was begun in the monastery.    Prior Crauden had a chapel
built, adjoining his house, which is still named after him.    The
chapel is small and stands over an undercroft which was converted
into another chapel for the use of the scholars at the Kings' School
in 1935.    The upper part is a gem of Decorated architecture, though
the carving has been sadly defaced.    It is fortunate to have survived
at all, for Cromwell's Commissioners in 1649 scheduled it for
destruction and the materials to be sold for the estimated amount
of £33  17s.    It was saved by becoming a dwelling house.    One
of the interesting features is the floor of medieval tiles, many
of which still retain their glaze.    There is a picture of Adam and
Eve on the floor of the sanctuary and a border of heraldic lions
round the main part of the floor.

The great gate of the monastery, known as Ely Porta, was
begun during this period, 1396-7, in the reign of Richard II, but
was not finished for some time, and it seems that the original design
was not adhered to as being too expensive.    All the later work is
of a rougher nature and the vault in the archway has not been
finished.    It was often known as Walpol's Gate, from the name of
the prior who was concerned with its erection.    It was the work of
John Meppushal, a master mason who had previously done work
at Cambridge and afterwards built the octagonal top to the west
tower of the Cathedral.    The gate is still closed at night, and the
College, as the former monastic property is called, is patrolled by
a watchman.    The room on the left, as one enters the Porta, was
once a prison.    The original door is preserved in the south porch
of the Cathedral.    The upper part of the Porta is now used by the
Kings' School for class rooms and meetings.

Another building of this period is the Painted Chamber, which
occupies the upper part of the building with a turret which projects
northwards from the Infirmary.    It was supposed to be the residence of Alan of Walsingham and was also used as a place where
monks could meet their friends or relatives.    Like all the remaining
monastic buildings it is now used as one of the canonry houses, or
part of the Kings' School.

In addition to these building works, Alan of Walsingham conducted the business affairs of the monastery, and there are records
of purchases of property in Stepil Row, now known as High Street,

and at Braham, on the main road to Cambridge, about a mile outside the city.

Mr. R. E. Swartwout, in his book *The Monastic Craftsman*, sets out to disprove the theory that the monks in the Middle Ages did their own building and made the ornaments of their churches; but he admits that Alan of Walsingham was trained as a goldsmith and that he had greater qualifications than the ordinary sacrist for superintending the building of the Octagon. He had the assistance of good master masons and a master carpenter who constructed the Lantern and doubtless they were responsible for the technical side of the work, if not for the conception of the whole.

Alan is believed to be buried beneath a slab at the east end of the nave at the point which was the entrance to his new Choir. His epitaph is said to call him "The flower of craftsmen."

# CHAPTER VIII

# Ely in the Fifteenth Century

So far, it has not been possible to form a clear picture of the city of Ely as it was in early times. Apart from the monastic buildings and the church there is nothing standing which can be older than the Tudor period, but we are fortunate in having, in the British Museum, a detailed survey of the city which was taken in the fourth year of the reign of King Henry V, which was either 1416 or 1417, according to our method of reckoning dates; that is, about the time of the Battle of Agincourt and Joan of Arc.

This survey gives the names and measurements of every property in the city, and the name of its occupant, so is of great value. It is interesting to see how little the city has changed in its lay-out, and how most of the names have been handed down, if not till the present day, at least until within the memory of the older in-habitants who are still alive.

The survey began at the High Bridge. The first field on the right after crossing the bridge towards the city was known as Briggemead, and provided part of the income of the Bridge Reeve who was in charge of the High Bridge; the office of Bridge Reeve is now held by the Organist of the Cathedral and the income from the field augments his stipend. Coming towards the city the street now known as Annesdale was then Auntresdale. A stream then flowed under the main road at a point near the present Angel Inn and the bridge which crossed it was known as Stonbrigge or Castelbrigge. The open space opposite the gas works was called Castelhithe. The present Potter's Lane was then The Potteries. In Potter's Lane was a tenement known as Duffhousyerd, a name obviously meaning Dove House Yard. Large dove cotes, which housed numbers of pigeons, were common adjuncts to manor houses and other establishments in the middle ages, and were an important source of food. The birds would eat other people's grain, so that the cost to their owner for fattening them for the table was little or nothing. This particular dove cote was left to the monastery by Robert Huderyer.

Opposite Potter's Lane is Broad Street, known as Broad Lane in the Survey. The names of the little lanes which lead from Broad Street to the river appear to have changed. In those days, and in fact till the coming of the railway, this part of Ely was the most important, commercially, as most goods were brought by water.

There were hithes, or landing places, with warehouses which were a source of revenue to the monks, particularly during the annual fairs. To-day some of the fair-ground vehicles find room for parking in this neighbourhood, while their owners are occupied upon the Market Place. The Fairs date back to the foundation of the bishopric in the early part of the 12th century. St. Audrey's (Etheldreda's) Fair is always held at the time of her festival and there is also the May Fair. In early times fairs provided an opportunity for the country people to do their shopping, but now they have degenerated into commercialized amusements.

The origin of the word "tawdry" is connected with St. Audrey's Fair, for it is a shortening of the Saint's name which became associated with the cheap brightly-coloured silken necklaces which were known as Etheldreda's chains.

Continuing the tour round the city and following the route taken by the 15th century Surveyor we find that the prior's vineyard was on the southern side of the present Park, adjoining Back Hill and Broad Street. The land still known as The Vineyards which lies to the north-east of the Market Place is the site of the bishop's vineyard of medieval times. The entrance to the original vineyard was probably from what is now known as Fore Hill, halfway between Lisle Lane and the Market Place. Lisle Lane was then called Lile's Lane, from de l'Isle, the name of the owner of the property. Bray's Lane commemorates the medieval family of de Bray, who owned a manor and were apparently wealthy, for the monastery borrowed money from Isabella de Bray. The family was related to the Salamon family who have already been mentioned, and through them probably to Alan of Walsingham.

The lane still known as Butcher's Row which runs between the backs of the buildings in the High Street and Market Street was known as The Butchery, and must have looked rather like the famous Shambles at York with open-fronted booths for shops. Market Street was known until recently as Gaol Street from the bishop's Gaol which still stands at the junction with Lynn Road. It is not mentioned in the Survey. Newnham Street cuts through a district which bore that name in the 15th century. Nutholt Lane was then known as Schendeforth or Shendeforde Lane. Until recent times it was called Red Cross Street in memory of a red calvary which stood at its junction with Lynn Road, and until the present century Nutholt Lane was the entrance to the city. The red cross was probably destroyed at the time of the Reformation. It must have been like the way-side crosses still to be seen in continental countries.

The continuation of Shendeforde Lane is now Egremont Street, which was then called Akyrman Street, the present name appearing to be a corruption.   Various forms of the name are Akermanstrete, Agemanstrete and Egreman Street, the last being the name in the 1860's.   It was evidently part of the Roman road which ran from Cambridge to Littleport.

St. Mary's Street is not named in the Survey but appears to have been the northern boundary of "le Grene," now Palace Green. Except for the Chantry, which was founded by Bishop Northwold in the early 13th century for four chaplains to pray for the repose of the souls of the bishops and monks of Ely, the other buildings bordering the Green and the south side of St. Mary's Street must be later encroachments.   The original Chantry has long since gone, but the eighteenth-century house, which stands on the site and bears the name acts as a reminder.

To the west of St. Mary's Church, where the Almshouses stand at present, was the Sacrist's, or Sextry, Barn, which was not pulled down till 1842.   It was 291 feet long by 39 feet wide, and careful drawings were made of it before it was destroyed.   Silver Street, which leads from St. Mary's Street to the Ely Porta, or Walpol's Gate, as it was then known, is given two names in the Survey, Swalugh Lane and Walpool's Lane.   Church Lane, which runs into it, was known by its present name.

High Street was known as Stepil Row from a steeple connected with one of the entrance gates of the Priory.   The picturesque timbered house which spans one of the present openings, is often known as Steeple Gate still, though more frequently as Snell's archway.

Several place-names in Ely are the names of persons which have become attached to the property they inhabited.   One such name was Kilby's Corner; the house on the south side of High Street opposite the Lamb Hotel.   Another was Mepsale's Corner at the junction of Downham Road with St. Mary's Street.   John Mepsale had a house there in 1416.   Perhaps he was the John Meppushal who built the Porta.   Evidently the habits of our medieval fore-fathers in naming places were similar to our own.   One wonders whether modern applications of the same principle will survive as long as some of these old names which were used for nearly five hundred years.

During the 15th century agricultural land in many parts of the country began to be enclosed in order to make it suitable for sheep farming and this caused great distress.   People who had made a living from working in the fields not only found themselves without work but the amount of food produced fell as well.

Villages became depopulated and small units of land were amalgamated to form larger ones—a policy which we see in action again
in the present day, and for the same reason: more economical working.    An Act of Parliament was passed in 1488 ordering all enclosed
land to be thrown open again, and a systematic enquiry was made
into the matter.    Evidently this did not have much effect for in
1548 there were risings of which Kett's Rebellion in Norfolk is
one of the best known.

Between 1486 and 1548 official surveys of enclosures in Cambridgeshire were made and these give us details of the various
holdings in and around Ely, their size and who occupied them.
They also mention complaints of lanes or "droves" being stopped
up by farmers and that land which "was wont to lye open with the
fields and the tenants of Ely had always shak and Comon in the
same".    "Shak" usually means the run of the fields between
harvest and seed time.    There does not seem to be much evidence
of sheep farming round Ely except in the direction of Soham, and
there Symeon Stuard, brother of the first Dean of Ely and great
uncle of Oliver Cromwell's mother, made himself unpopular by
enclosing land for farming sheep.    Other enclosures in Ely appear
to have been for dairy farming which, while providing less work
for the people did not reduce the food supply.

Many of the names of places in 1548 were very similar to those by
which they are known to-day and some, Redmore, Newnham and
Hall Farm are the same.

It is interesting to note that the plan of the city has changed so
little in five hundred years.    In fact until after the Great War of
1914-18 very little development took place.    Since then building
has covered the New Barns Estate and spread along Lynn Road,
Downham Road, Cambridge and Barton Roads. and elsewhere.
Unfortunately it has largely taken the form of "ribbon development," so that public services have to be taken a long way to the
outlying houses and the people who live in them have to go a mile
or more to the centre of the city and nearly double that distance
to the railway station.

At the time of the 15th century Survey most of the houses were
probably built of wood and plaster.    The shops were open-
fronted booths, some only of a temporary character and used by
merchants at the time of the fairs.    Some old cottages which
remained in Broad Street were removed as recently as 1933, but
they may have belonged to the 16th or 17th centuries.

Sometimes very ordinary looking brick houses will disclose
massive timbers when their interiors are examined, and it is probable
that many old houses have been refaced with brick to make them

42

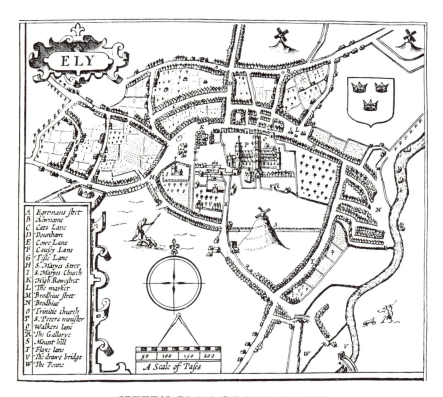

A Scale of Pasce

SPEED'S PLAN OF ELY IN 1610

This illustration appears by kind permission of the Trustees of the British Museum where the original is to be found, and also by courtesy of Cambridge University Press from the reproduction in T. D. Atkinson's *Architectural History of the Benedictine Monastery of St. Etheldreda at Ely.*

# Speed's Plan of Ely in 1610

This plan of Ely appears in Speed's *The Theatre of the Empire of Great Britaine* in the corner of the map of the county of Hunting-donshire and was published in 1611. It will be seen that the extent of the city at that date was almost the same as it was three hundred years later. The list of street names does show a number of differences. In the cases of Egremont Street, Newnham Street, St. Mary's Street, The Market Place, and The Gallery the names are the same with only the inevitable variations of spelling. One mistake seems apparent as (D) is given as Dounham instead of the present Lynn Road. Trinitie church was known by that name until it once again became the Lady Chapel of the Cathedral in 1938, but "S. Peters minster" seems a surprising name for the Cathedral, but it reminds us that the dedication was to St. Peter and St. Etheldreda. Cherry hill is called Mount hill, but it did not receive its present name till after it was raised and planted with trees by James Bentham in the 18th century. It will be noticed that the eastern end of St. Mary's Street (K) was named High Rowestret. Originally there were houses only on the northern side and these looked across the green towards the Bishop's Palace. The buildings on the south side of this part of the street and those bordering Palace Green are encroachments of which the earliest was the Chantry. Street names which have changed completely are (C) Cats Lane, (E) Cowe Lane, (T) flaxe lane, which are now respectively Chapel Street, West Fen Road and Broad Street; Causey Lane which is possibly the same as Hills Lane and (G) Tisse Lane, which seems rather obscure and would appear to be where Chiefs Street is now. Fore Hill and Quayside were respectively (M) Brodhiue street and (N) Brodhiue (otherwise Broadhythe): and Silver Street was (Q) Walkers lane. It will be noticed that Lynn Road, although not named beyond the corner of Egremont Street, is shown to have a number of closely packed houses where few old houses now survive and houses extend along Prickwillow Road almost as far as at present. Although there are obvious inaccuracies as witnessed by the omission of buildings still standing which date back before the date of the plan, it is obviously a reasonably good guide to the state of the city in the early 17th century.

"up-to-date." Part of the premises occupied by the author, which were known to date back to about 1700, was found to be built of wattle and daub, although there was no hint of this sort of construction to be gathered from the appearance of the exterior. The old wall consisted of split sticks, still retaining their bark, tied together with hemp to form a kind of lattice and the whole coated with mud. A timber frame must have taken the weight of the upper storey.

Practically all building in Ely during the last three centuries has been of brick, the older kind being delightfully variegated in colour, but as time went on bricks became standardised to a dark shade of yellow, and recently to a lighter shade of yellow or red.

There are the remains of a brick kiln, which supplied the neighbourhood, at Littleport, five miles from Ely. A curious local form of construction is to be observed in the gables of houses in the district, which have wedge-shaped insertions of bricks laid at an angle to the horizontal. This has a slightly decorative effect, but is supposed to be for strengthening purposes. The soft earth of the fens does not provide a firm foundation and many houses sink, very often at an angle. Modern houses are built on concrete rafts which spread the weight of the building over a larger surface.

# CHAPTER IX

# The Last Days of the Monastery

AFTER the great building operations of the time of Alan of Walsingham very little was done to the Cathedral. A number of windows were altered to conform with the newer style and so admit more light. There were minor repairs and alterations necessitated by changing conditions, but there was little need for great works and in any case the cost of building had increased as a result of the shortage of labour produced by the Black Death.

One important work was done during the 15th century, namely, the erection of the upper part of the west tower, though it is very difficult to determine, from the scanty records available, when this was done. Apparently there was a short spire at the top of the Norman tower and this was removed and the present octagonal structure with its four detached corner turrets erected. A short slender spire was placed above this. From the start, this 64 foot high masonry storey seems to have given trouble although it was made as light as possible to avoid overloading the tower, and trussed inside with a wooden frame to make it secure. Already in 1345-6 six very heavy bells were placed in the tower and the combined weight and vibration gave great anxiety for some years. Apparently the weight was too much for the foundations, because four massive arches had to be inserted inside the existing Transitional Norman ones, in order to strengthen them. If we look up upon entering the west end of the Cathedral we can see the tops of the older arches showing above the pointed Perpendicular work. This work was done about 1474-1478 mainly at the expense of Bishop Grey, who also gave ornaments and windows to the Cathedral.

The Perpendicular style of architecture was the last development of Gothic architecture in England. It is not found on the Continent where a more florid style developed and where, at the same period, the effects of the Renaissance were already being felt. The main features are the vertical lines from which it gets its name, and horizontal lines which combine with them to give an effect of panelling. In windows these lines are named transoms and mullions respectively. They are repeated on wall surfaces, sometimes to give greater apparent height to the windows. Carved decoration became plainer than in the preceding Decorated period, and was often heraldic in character, though very fine foliage sculpture is sometimes found, notably at King's College, Cambridge. The Perpendicular period lasted for about a hundred and fifty years—longer than either of the previous styles of architecture which have been mentioned.   Apart from the arches beneath the west tower, the examples of Perpendicular work at Ely are not notable, except in Bishop Alcock's Chapel, which has a fan-vaulted ceiling—the final stage in the development of this style.

There is uncertainty regarding the fate of the north-west transept. It either collapsed or was removed about the same time as the work was done on the tower, but whether before or after is not known. The great buttress which takes part of the thrust formerly sustained by the north-west transept is of 15th century workmanship.   Typical Perpendicular decoration is to be seen upon it.

The Cathedral now presented the appearance which it retained for three hundred years until the spire was removed in 1799. There are good many engravings and pictures to be seen showing the spire and the Octagon and Lantern in the state before their restoration, or rather completion, by Sir G. G. Scott.   As left by Alan of Walsingham there were no elaborate pinnacles of stone round the top of the Octagon, and the design of the lead work on the Lantern was different.   The frontispiece to this volume taken from Bentham's *History and Antiquities of the Cathedral Church of Ely* shows the appearance of the building as it was in 1756.

Inside the building are two notable memorial chapels built to the memory of Bishop Alcock, the founder of Jesus College, Cambridge, and to Bishop West.   The former represents the culmination of the Gothic style of building in England and the latter the beginnings of the Renaissance style which came in with the Tudors.   Bishop Alcock's Chapel is built of clunch most elaborately carved with much undercutting and delicate detail and a pendent boss of the fan vaulting type.   Miss M. D. Anderson suggests that the Bishop's taste for exotic ornament may have been formed when he was ambassador at the Court of Castile in 1470.

Bishop West was laid to rest in his beautiful chapel in 1534. Although it is still Gothic in form, most of the decoration and detail is in the Renaissance style.   Some of this work was done by Italian workmen who were largely employed in England at this time by the wealthy builders of great houses.   Bishop West was not only Bishop of Ely, but was employed by King Henry VIII upon diplomatic missions.   He lived in greater state than any other Bishop of Ely.   A hundred servants attended him, and two hundred poor were fed daily at his palace gates.

Bishop West's successor was Bishop Goodrich, a reformer and supporter of Henry VIII in his divorce proceedings against

Catharine of Aragon. He was also one of the chief agents for the dissolution of the monasteries, an act which had a serious effect on the social life of the whole country.

Ely, like all other monasteries, was dissolved; but on account of the bishop's connection with it, the monks suffered less than most of their brethren elsewhere. The Cathedral and most of the monastery buildings were allowed to survive, but in 1541 Bishop Goodrich issued an order "that all Images, Relics, Shrines, etc., be so totally demolished and obliterated that no remains or memory be found of them." It is probable that it was at this time that the beautiful carvings in the Lady Chapel were defaced.

The change, as we have seen, did not affect Ely so much as some other places. The Prior of the monastery became the first Dean of the newly created Chapter. Three of the eight newly appointed Canons were former monks, as were six out of the eight new Minor Canons. There were eight singing men, now known as Lay Clerks, and a number of Bedesmen provided for in the statutes of the Dean and Chapter. A survey of the buildings, which still exists, was made by Henry VIII's commissioners in 1531. It gives a good picture of the monastic buildings as they were at that date and also outlines their future uses.

Although the monastery had been built to accommodate seventy monks it had scarcely ever been full and the numbers had, at times, fallen to less than thirty; seven years before the dissolution the number was only thirty-six besides the Prior. The income of the monastery from rents of property, etc., at the time of the dissolution was between £1,000 and £1,300 according to different estimates. This translated into modern money would be a much greater figure.

Bishop Goodrich was not entirely destructive, for he built the long gallery of the Bishop's Palace. On the lower part of the oriel window in the middle of this gallery are two plaster panels, now sadly defaced by the action of the weather, one of which recites the Duties of Man to God, and the other his Duties towards his Neighbour.

Bishop Goodrich is buried in the Cathedral under a fine brass slab showing him, rather ironically, dressed in the full vestments for the Mass which he had helped to suppress.

Bishop Goodrich's superior in the spoilation of the monasteries was Thomas Cromwell, Henry VIII's Minister, and it is interesting at this point to mention him because of his connection with Oliver Cromwell, who will appear at a later date in the history of Ely. The great-grandfather of Oliver was named Richard Williams and was nephew to Thomas Cromwell, but out of courtesy to his uncle took the name of Cromwell and was virtually adopted by him. He shared in the spoils of the monastic suppression and received the estates of Ramsey Abbey, St. Neot's Priory, Hinchinbrooke Nunnery, and a house of Austin Canons at Huntingdon. It was at this last house that Oliver was born and lived during his boyhood.

In a similar manner Robert Steward, the last Prior and first Dean of Ely, has some bearing on the future history of the Cathedral, for his elder brother was the other great-grandfather of Oliver Cromwell. Dean Steward traced his family back to the Stuarts, the Royal Family of Scotland, but his claim has been disproved, and it is alleged that the origin of his name was Sty-ward or Pig-keeper. Browne Willis, who saw the Cathedral before the alterations made in the 18th century, gives the spelling of the Dean's name on his grave stone as Styward. In the south choir aisle are some Steward tombs with elaborate coats of arms showing many quarterings based on the claims of the Dean. Some of Dean Steward's experiments with heraldry are drawn in the margins of old manuscripts and books in the Cathedral Library. He also had a habit of writing his name in old books.

Following the Protestant persecution under Edward VI came the reactionary persecution by the Catholics under Mary. Although the district did not suffer so much as some places, two Protestants were burnt at the stake at Ely. They were William Wolsey and Robert Pigot, both of Wisbech, and their offence was calling the Sacrament of the Altar "an idol."

Upon the death of Queen Mary, Elizabeth abolished the authority of the Papacy in England and seized the whole of the property of the Bishops of Ely, handing back only a portion of it to the new bishop, Bishop Cox, who was later made to give up Ely House, Holborn, which had been the London residence of the Bishops of Ely. In 1575 Cox actually incurred the Queen's displeasure by boldly refusing to further alienations of the revenues of the see. From the death of Bishop Cox in 1580 (whose funeral is the subject of a curious picture, painted in reverse, still preserved in the Bishop's House at Ely) till the appointment of his successor in 1600, the Queen devoted the whole of the income of the see to her own benefit.

*Plate 12*

THE PALACE

*Plate* 13 THE GRANARY

*Plate* 14 THE PORTA

Plate 15 ST. MARY'S CHURCH AND CROMWELL HOUSE

Plate 16 THE HOSPITAL OF ST. JOHN

*Plate* 17                                 CHERRY HILL

*Plate* 18     THE STEEPLE GATE

## CHAPTER X

# Oliver Cromwell and Ely

THE 17th century began quietly at Ely. Life in the College, as the remains of the former monastery were now called, had fallen into a peaceful routine which was maintained until the present day. In spite of the fact that Cambridge and East Anglia had taken kindly to the reformed religion, Ely had a succession of "High Church" bishops, and except for the period of the Civil War, incense was used up till the 18th century and was then given up, not for doctrinal reasons, but because it irritated the respiratory system of one of the Minor Canons!

The second of these Jacobean bishops was Lancelot Andrewes, a saintly man, whose books are still read for devotional purposes. He was followed in 1619 by Bishop Nicholas Felton, who was one of the translators of the "Authorised Version" of the Bible. Another "High Church" bishop was Matthew Wren. He was so highly in favour with Charles I that it is said that Archbishop Laud was jealous of him. He was imprisoned by the Parliamentarians in 1641 with other bishops, for protesting against their exclusion from the House of Lords. He was not popular, even among people who were in agreement with his religious views. In a time when liberality in entertaining was a measure of a man's standing he failed through his meanness, and he is said to have left the Bishop's Palace in a state of disrepair.

An early 17th century dean was Henry Caesar, whose lifelike monument can be seen close to the pulpit in the Cathedral. He was a lover of good music and encouraged this aspect of worship in the Cathedral. He "left 1000 *l.* to augment the Vicar's and singing Men's Places, but it not having been laid out in Lands, and the Choir being put down in 1645, his Heirs would not pay the Interest of it after the Restauration of the Church and Monarchy, and so it was lost." The quotation is from Browne Willis.

If things were quiet in ecclesiastical circles there was unrest among the inhabitants of Fenland, which still remained in the state which William the Conqueror found it six hundred years before. The draining of the fens in medieval times had been a matter of local concern, but during the latter years of the reign of Queen Elizabeth large scale plans were discussed and an Act of Parliament was passed in 1600 to implement them. The fen people opposed these schemes, as they knew that they would alter their way of life and take away the living they had made from fishing and wild-fowling. Although they must have known that labour would be required for farming the reclaimed land, they were of an independent nature and had not been used to working for other men. Besides these objections the owners of the land were faced with the difficulty of financing the work, and they were allowed to contract with "undertakers" who promised to do the drainage work in return for a specified acreage of the reclaimed land.

King James I took a lively interest in the draining of the fens. There was a great deal of planning and many complaints during his reign, but nothing was done. At last he declared that he would become an undertaker himself with a reward of 120,000 acres for doing the work. The Dutch engineer Vermuyden was called in to report on the matter, but owing to the death of the King in 1625, no progress was made. Five years later, Francis Russell, Earl of Bedford, undertook to make what is now known as the Bedford Level, "good summer land" within six years. He was joined by thirteen other Adventurers, so-called because they "adventured" their capital in the scheme. Vermuyden was given the task and work on a large scale began at last.

Vermuyden's system was to make straight canals in order to take the water to the sea by the shortest route. His chief work was the Old Bedford River, which stretches in a straight line for twenty-one miles from Earith in Huntingdonshire to Denver in Norfolk.

It is here that Oliver Cromwell enters into the story of Ely. We have seen that he was born at Huntingdon, where his father was a farmer. He was at Sidney Sussex College, Cambridge, when his father died in 1617, and he returned home at the age of eighteen, without taking a degree, to manage his land and rule the household, consisting of his mother and six sisters. After a few years at Huntingdon he sold his farm and moved to St. Ives, where he took up grazing, and in 1638 he moved to Ely to the house which now serves as the Vicarage. It was the property of Oliver's uncle, Sir Thomas Steward, who had died leaving it to his nephew.

Cromwell became one of the governors of Parsons' Charity, which still carries on good work in the city; the almshouses which stand on the ground adjoining Cromwell's House are one of the means by which they care for the poor of Ely.

Cromwell had already been Member of Parliament for Hunting-don for some years but upon moving to Ely he was made member for Cambridge. It was in his capacity as M.P. that he successfully opposed the action of the Earl of Bedford's company which had tried to claim the land as their reward before completing the work of drainage. Cromwell was in agreement with the principle of draining the fens, but wished to defend the rights of the people who would be deprived of their livelihood as a result. In 1638 a number of men from Ely broke down dykes at Whelpmore under cover of a football match.

Four years after Cromwell took up residence at Ely the Civil War began, but the services in the Cathedral went on unhindered until January 164¾, when, according to Carlyle, Cromwell as Governor of Ely "made a transient appearance in the cathedral one day, memorable to the Reverend Mr. Hitch and us". He had already written to Mr. Hitch, requiring him "to forbear altogether the choir service, so unedifying and offensive, lest the soldiers should in any tumultuary or disorderly way attempt the reformation of the cathedral church." Mr. Hitch paid no attention, and Cromwell accordingly appeared in time of service, "with rabble at his heels, and with his hat on," and ordered the "assembly" to leave the cathedral. Mr. Hitch paused for a moment, but soon recommenced: when 'Leave off your fooling, and come down, Sir,' said Cromwell; in a voice still audible to this editor; "which Mr. Hitch did now instantaneously give ear to." Cromwell locked the door of the cathedral, put the key in his pocket and the building remained closed for seventeen years. Fortunately the building survived this long period of neglect as a result of the care which had been taken of the fabric in the past by the Dean and Chapter.

During the Civil War, Cromwell was coming and going a great deal, and at one time was ordered by Parliament to conduct the defence of Cambridgeshire from Ely. In 1645 the Royalists came as close as Huntingdon, and many Parliamentarian refugees came to Ely for safety, thus following the tradition of the place which had sheltered Hereward and his Saxons, and later the Barons. It is interesting to note in passing that once again, in the present day, it has provided a safe haven for victims of the Nazi persecution and for children evacuated from London. Cromwell was proud of his Governorship of Ely, and said, "I will make the Isle of Ely the strongest place in the world," and "I will make it a place for God to dwell in."

The work of draining the fens had fallen into abeyance during the Civil Wars, but when the Protectorate became established Cromwell caused the work to be continued and appointed Vermuyden as engineer once again. A large number of Scots prisoners who had been captured at the Battle of Dunbar, and Dutchmen taken by Admiral Blake were employed upon the work. Some of them were housed in Wisbech Castle, a former palace of the Bishops of Ely. A second Bedford River was cut parallel with, and about half a mile from, the Old Bedford River. It is known as the "Hundredfoot" from its width, the Old Bedford River being seventy feet wide. At flood time the water can cover the whole of the area between the two rivers and this land is known as the "Washes."

The results of the drainage work were good and crops were grown on the reclaimed land; but it was soon found that the surface of the ground began to sink and it was necessary to pump the water from the ditches and dykes up to the higher level of the main drains and rivers. Windmills were used for this purpose but were not very satisfactory. In 1820 the first steam pump was installed and the engine house with its tall chimney soon became a familiar feature of the fen landscape. Diesel engines are now taking the place of steam, but great problems still face the drainage engineers.

In 1646 Parliament voted Cromwell an estate worth £2,500 a year, and this enabled him to move from Ely to London where, for the future, his work mainly lay.

Cromwell's association with the district did not cease, for most of his family are buried in the church at Wicken, a few miles from Ely. Strangely enough, it is in this parish that the only remaining portion of the fen remains in its original undrained state, and a visit shows something of the appearance of the remainder of the district before Cromwell's time. Richard Cromwell, son of Oliver and "Lord Protector" for a short time after his death, lived in retirement at Wicken after he was deposed at the restoration of Charles II, and it is said that Charles once visited him there.

# CHAPTER XI

# Ely after the Civil War

In 1638, shortly before the commencement of the Civil War, Matthew Wren was made Bishop of Ely, being translated from the see of Norwich, where he had been very unpopular among the rather Puritan element in Norfolk. In 1641 he protested, with other bishops, against their exclusion from the House of Lords and was sent with them to the Tower. He was set at liberty for a short time in 1642, but again arrested and imprisoned for eighteen years, being released and restored to his see at the Restoration of Charles II. As a thankoffering he built the chapel at Pembroke Hall, Cambridge which was designed by his famous nephew Sir Christopher Wren. During his imprisonment Bishop Wren used what influence he could for the good of his diocese. On his return there was naturally a good deal to be done and, with the aid of his son, who was Archdeacon, he conducted "visitations" or enquiries in every parish of his diocese in order to re-establish good order and see that the churches were properly equipped.

The Cathedral was opened for services once again, and, as we have seen, it had stood its long period of neglect well. Little work had to be done to the fabric, but the north wall of the nave was refaced in 1662, where the Church of St. Cross had stood against it more than a century before. The windows of the north aisle at this point are the old mullions and tracery from the Church of St. Cross and date from the 14th century. The former monastic buildings had not fared so well. During the Protectorate some of them had been stripped of their lead roofs and had become too ruinous to be repaired. One building which suffered in this way was the library of the Dean and Chapter. It had not been the library of the monks, having been built about 1550 after the suppression of the Monastery. It is strange that no trace or mention of an earlier library can be found. It is presumed that the books were kept in the Cloister and there is an alcove at the side of the South Door of the Cathedral which is known to have been made to house books in the 14th century. The present day library is housed in the eastern portion of the south transept. It contains thousands of books on a variety of subjects and many of them are three or four hundred years old. The more valuable manuscripts, deeds, charters, etc., some of which have come down from Saxon times, and in many cases bear the seals and signatures of kings of England, are housed in a muniment room over the archway leading into the College from the High Street.

It was in 1649 that a survey of the College buildings was made by the Parliamentary Commissioners which resulted in a good deal of damage being done. We have seen in an earlier chapter that Prior Crauden's Chapel was scheduled for demolition, but was saved by being converted into a dwelling house.

The iron-work on the west doors inside the Galilee Porch reminds us of Bishop Wren, for small wrens are included in the design.

The bishop who followed Bishop Wren in 1667 was Bishop Benjamin Laney, whose name is still remembered in the city in connection with Bishop Laney's Charity, which provides the funds for apprenticing boys to tradesmen. At the time of his being bound to the apprenticeship each boy is presented with a Bible. Bishop Laney was followed by Bishop Peter Gunning (1675-1684), whose tomb can be seen in the Cathedral. It is one of only eight tombs of this period which show bishops wearing mitres. Bishop Gunning was one of the chief revisers of the Prayer Book of 1662 and composed the well-known "Prayer for all Sorts and Conditions of Men." His successor was Bishop Francis Turner, who was one of the seven bishops prosecuted by James II for refusing to countenance his second Declaration of Indulgence in 1687.

During this period the central portion of the Bishop's Palace was built. It links the two towers built by Bishop Alcock, and contains large and lofty rooms overlooking pleasant grounds in the middle of which stands perhaps the largest and oldest plane tree in England. It was planted in the 17th century and rises to a great height, though, like the Palace, it is dwarfed by the tower of the Cathedral.

On the 29th March, 1699, at 10 o'clock in the evening, the north-western corner of the north transept of the Cathedral fell down. It was rebuilt from the designs of Sir Christopher Wren, the famous architect of St. Paul's Cathedral, and a nephew of Bishop Wren. The work was done under the supervision of Grumbold, Sir Christopher's assistant at St. Paul's, and cost £2,637 6s. 4d. It is easy to see from the outside which is Wren's work, not only from the different texture of the stonework and the narrower joints than can be found in the surrounding Norman work, but also because of the difference in the style. It is an imitation of the Norman work as seen through the eyes of a man living in the 17th century. Notice how one of the round-headed windows has stone transoms and mullions, which were never used by Norman builders. It is generally agreed that the doorway in the Tuscan style is out of place. It looks like a piece of St. Paul's Cathedral in the wrong setting.

Another piece of work of the same period is the doorway leading into the part of the cloister which now forms the south porch. It makes no pretence to copy an earlier style and thus does not offend the eye in the same way as the work in the north transept. Earlier in the book we saw that each period produced its own style of architecture and that the styles blend successfully, but in the case of the earler additions no attempt was made to copy an out-moded style in the way which Wren did.

Soon after the work on the north transept was done, there was a famous hurricane which swept England on 26th November, 1704. Ely was only on the fringe of the storm, but much of the lead on the roof of the Cathedral was torn off; forty windows were blown out, and there was other damage. Damage to the Cathedral amounted to £2,000 while the damage in the city was estimated at £20,000.

To the early 18th century belong some of the houses which give character to the city. The Chantry facing the Palace has already been mentioned and the two other houses on the same side of the Green belong to the same period. The fine house in the north-east corner of the Market Place, which is known as Archer House, is also a product of the 18th century; behind it is a walled garden with a summer house which figures in old prints of Ely, for it stands up boldly above the roofs of the houses further down the hill. Needham's School on Back Hill was founded in 1734; a tablet on the front of the building gives particulars of the bequest.

Brick had by this time become the usual material for building in the district and variegated tiles were used for roofs. It is interesting to look down on Ely from the upper parts of the Cathedral from which it is easy to pick out the older buildings by the material of which their roofs are made. The more modern buildings are roofed with slate or mass-produced tiles.

A picturesque part of Ely which dates from the latter part of the 18th century is the district known as Waterside. The houses, which were once the residences of Ely merchants, have descended in the social scale but still have a quiet dignity, and, as very little traffic penetrates to this *cul-de-sac*, it is easy to visualise the past when one looks at them. In the days when they were built, waterways were still the chief means of transport. In 1753 a boat for the conveyance of passengers and goods left Cambridge for Ely every Tuesday and Friday, returning the next day. The distance of twenty miles was covered in six hours.

The work of draining the fens continued, and in fact is never finished. A Corporation of Conservators of the Fens was constituted in 1664; it continues to maintain the banks in good order, clear dykes, and do whatever is necessary to drain the Great Level, as the basin of the River Cam is called. Just inside the south entrance to the Cathedral is a large memorial tablet, removed from the Lady Chapel in 1938, which was erected by an admirer, to the memory of a Mr. Humphrey Smith, who died on 27th March, 1743. It records that he was a drainage engineer who did good work in the district, particularly in cutting Smith's Leam from Guyhirne to Peterborough.

Daniel Defoe, the author of *Robinson Crusoe*, visited Ely in 1724, when writing his *Tour Through England and Wales*. He wrote as follows: "the town, when the minster, so they call it is described, everything remarkable is said that there is room to say; and of the minster that is the most remarkable thing that I could hear, namely, that some of it is so antient, totters so much with every gust of wind, looks so like decay, and seems so near it, that when ever it does fall, all that 'tis likely will be thought strange in it, will be that it did not fall a hundred years sooner."

If Defoe did not devote much space to Ely he made up for it in his description of the wild-fowling industry which he described in great detail. The decoys, as the huge traps were called, were so profitable, that they were let for rents ranging from £100 to £500 a year. Decoy ducks were tamed and became accustomed to certain feeding grounds. They were then allowed to fly abroad, bringing back with them other ducks, which were enticed into large netted enclosures by means of food. When safely inside they were taken out and killed, but the decoy ducks either avoided the trap or were recognized and spared by their masters. At St. Ives, where the fowl was brought to be sent to London, Defoe was told that they generally sent up three thousand couple a week.

Defoe also describes the trade of conveying fish, chiefly tench, pike, perch and eels, in water butts by road to London, the water being changed at stopping places on the journey.

The people of Ely at this time evidently enjoyed a game which was popular in East Anglia until the early nineteenth century and which was probably of ancient origin. This was called "camping," and appears to have combined some of the features of Rugby football and the present American football game. The ball, which was about the size of a cricket ball was carried, and the object of the players was to get it to their own goal. The game was very rough and often degenerated into a free fight. Seven or nine "snotches," as the goals were called, had to be scored to complete a game, and this sometimes took two or three hours. The game was usually played with bare feet; if boots were worn it was called "savage camp." The name "camp" is supposed to be derived from the Anglo-Saxon word meaning "combat." The field where this game was played was known as "camping close"; hence the name of a modern house which stands in Downham Road on the site of the old "close."

# CHAPTER XII

# Mr. Essex saves the Cathedral

IN the last chapter we saw that in the time of Daniel Defoe the Cathedral was said to be in a dangerous condition; probably his informers were wiser than they knew. In 1750, in the time of Bishop Matthias Mawson, Mr. Essex, the architect of some of the colleges at Cambridge, was called in to make a thorough examination of the fabric. He found that the upper part of the Galilee Porch was in a bad condition and recommended its removal, but, although the work was actually started, the Dean and Chapter fortunately decided to spare this particularly fine piece of Early English architecture.

At the east end of the Cathedral Mr. Essex found that the upper part of the stone gable had been forced outwards two feet by the pressure of the roof. The roof, which was then constructed exactly as the roof of the nave now appears, was what is known as a trussed rafter roof. It was probably the widest in span of any of that type. After getting the East Front back into the perpendicular by means of screws, Mr. Essex constructed a fresh roof to the choir and presbytery on what is known as the queen post system, with enormous tie beams which stretch from one wall to the other. This work was begun in 1757, and took five years to complete. It is interesting to see the names of workmen employed on the job written in large letters on the beams. One name is dated 1760 and there are three dated 1768, while other workmen, up to the present day, have written their names, more or less elaborately, on the rafters. We are thus provided with evidence useful in the tracing of pedigrees, though few of these names are common in Ely to-day. In fact, one name has "London" after it, showing that labour was imported.

The most serious defect which Mr. Essex discovered was that the great timbers of the lantern were rotten and instead of the weight being borne by sixteen main beams, only half of them were sound.

It is almost impossible to describe in so many words the construction of the timber work in the Lantern, so the reader is referred to Plate 7 (*b*), taken from a model which is exhibited in the South Transept. It is sometimes possible to see the timbers at first hand if special permission can be obtained; and one can then see how Mr. Essex strengthened the rotten beams by bolting new pieces on either side of them and by adding fresh beams to take the weight.

At this time there still stood in the nave the ancient Norman pulpitum, or stone screen. The plan in Browne Willis's "Survey" shows that the screen occupied the whole of the bay of the nave nearest the Octagon. The western front was pierced by three doorways and ornamented with tiers of arcading. The eastern face had one opening into the choir which consisted of seventy of Alan of Walsingham's stalls placed across the Octagon. Two spiral staircases gave access to the top of the pulpitum on which the organ was built. Mr. Essex demolished this screen, but before he did so careful drawings were made of it. It is thought that the arcading and staircase in the south transept may perhaps be part of the remains; but as the shafts are shown in Browne Willis's plan, it is not safe to accept this theory.

Browne Willis's plan also shows the positions of all the principal tombs in the Cathedral before some of them were moved by Mr. Essex and later restorers. The High Altar stood in the first bay of Bishop Hotham's choir with his tomb behind it. Mr. S. Inskip Ladds, a former Surveyor to the Dean and Chapter, has advanced a theory that the structure at present standing on the north side of the Presbytery, and regarded as the remains of the Shrine of St. Etheldreda, is in reality part of Bishop Hotham's tomb. Bentham's History of the Cathedral bears out this theory in one of its illustrations. Mr. Essex moved the High Altar and the stalls to the extreme east end of Bishop Northwold's Presbytery in an attempt to place the choir in a less draughty position. One of the lay clerks had died through the cold; it must be remembered that there were no heating arrangements in those days. A new screen was erected in the second bay of the choir and the organ placed above it.

Mr. Essex made his survey of the fabric between 1750 and 1757, and the work he did was but the bare minimum required to preserve the building from complete decay. Though from the point of view of taste he has been criticized for what he did, we owe the preservation of the building to him.

The following description of the building in a letter of Bishop Charles Lyttleton of Carlisle dated July 1757 shows how necessary the work was.

". . . On thursday I went to Ely . . . The Cathedral, or Minster, as it is styled, is a very noble Fabrick and may for its dimensions be justly styled the fifth largest Church in the Kingdom, but for its

slovenly condition in which it lies and the meanness of fitting up
the Choir, etc., it is far inferior to every other Cathedral except
Carlisle (and most Parish Churches).   Tho' the Dean and Chapter
are rather poor than rich, yet the Bishopric is plentifully endowed,
and therefore one wonders to find little or nothing done by any
of the Prelates since the Restoration towards beautifying a Church
where they reside not only a Bishop but Prince, Ely See having
Palatinate Jurisdiction . . ."

There was at this time a revival of interest in Gothic architecture,
and in 1771, just after the above-mentioned alterations were completed, Bentham's *History and Antiquities of Ely Cathedral* was
published.   James Bentham was a Minor Canon of the Cathedral,
and later Canon.   His book is still regarded as one of the most
important ever written on the subject, and has formed the basis
for subsequent books.

Bentham's book was not his only legacy to Ely, for he planted
an avenue of trees along Lynn Road, of which a few only remain,
and erected an obelisk, a few yards beyond the corner of Lynton
Drive.   The obelisk records the fact that posterity and not the
donor would see the result of his gift.

That Mr. Essex's repairs were no more than such and could
not be regarded as a restoration of the building may be seen from
the following description by the Hon. John Byng, later Viscount
Torrington, who wrote in his diary of a visit to Ely on 5th July,
1790: "Now, perhaps, I was not in a humour to be pleased; for,
except the centre dome, what is there?   I think it a shabby, ill-kept,
edifice, I mean the inside, for the outside is very lofty, and fine,
only sadly disfigured by the northern side of the west front, being
down; the chapels are dawb'd over by a whiting; and the stalls
and altar are in paltry taste."   His comment on the conduct of the
service is not encouraging: "Perhaps I was neither fit for a Lt.-Col.
or a Bishop; for I am for high dress, subordination, forms and
discipline; as a churchman, I had endeavoured to imitate that great
and good prelate, Archbishop Laud; for without pomp, order, and
method, neither the priesthood, or parade will flourish; and was I
in my stall, or my pulpit, I wou'd call to an offender, as I wou'd
to an offender on a field day; dirty surplices, slurring over the
divine service, are surely more reprehensible than dirty gaiters,
and slovenly motions?

"The town is mean, to an extreme; for if any man chuses to
observe, he will find that castles, and religious houses were the
safeguards, and comforts of the country; those withdrawn, their
dependencies must decay; what must the decrease of genteel
residence occasion in the country?"

There follows Col. Byng's bill for a meal at the Lamb Inn:

| LAMB INN, ELY | | |
|---|---|---|
| Dinner & Ale ... | ... | 1/– |
| Wine ... | ... ... | 1/2 |
| | | 2/2 |

It was on August 10th of this year that Parson Woodforde, of Weston Longville, near Norwich, recorded in his famous diary that he met James Bentham, then 82 years of age, and his son Rev. James Bentham who was Rector of Bradenham in Norfolk. Woodforde says "Old Mr. Bentham was dressed in a black Cloth Gown and Cassock and a Crape Scarf—He played Cards without Spectacles and walks quite strong." Among Bentham's public spirited acts were proposals for making turnpike roads in the Isle of Ely and these were carried out under powers conferred by Act of Parliament in 1763, and a road was constructed between Ely and Cambridge.

Parson Woodforde met Bentham at the house of Mr. Du Quesne who was a Prebend of Ely and also held a living in Norfolk. On several occasions Mr. Du Quesne sent Woodforde presents of fish which came from Ely. On December 14th, 1786 Woodforde describes them as "a brace of fish, called Eel-Pouts, a small fish the size of a very small Whiting," and again on April 2nd, 1790 "A score fine Smelts" which he ate for dinner as it was Good Friday. This shows that Ely was evidently famous for its fish at that date.

During the later years of the 18th century the New Barns estate was occupied by Mr. Tattersall, the dealer in horses whose name is still associated with important sales of bloodstock at Newmarket. During this time the Prince Regent sometimes stayed with Mr. Tattersall. Highflyer Farm was named after a famous racehorse.

The 18th century ended with the removal of the spire which surmounted the west tower, which, judging from old prints, did not add to the beauty of the structure.

# CHAPTER XIII

## Ely in the Early Nineteenth Century

THE turn of the century brought more unhappiness to the people of Ely. From 1793, for over twenty years, the Napoleonic Wars raged in Europe and England was for years under the constant threat of invasion. There was a plan to flood the fens in the event of an invasion by Napoleon in order to make the Isle of Ely a place of refuge once again. We read that John Gurney of Earlham, Norwich, and father of Elizabeth Fry the prison reformer, intended to evacuate his family to Ely if the French landed. Added to this, new acts for the enclosure of land were brought in; the common land which had been at the disposal of the country labourer for tilling and grazing was fenced and declared private property. The price of corn rose, but agricultural workers' wages did not rise with it. The condition of the people was desperate, and in 1816, after the Battle of Waterloo, the peasantry at Littleport took up arms. They sacked some of the houses of the more well-to-do and levied contributions on others and then marched to Ely armed with guns, pistols, scythes, etc. A waggon on which were mounted four punt guns—very formidable weapons —formed a conspicuous feature of the procession. The leading inhabitants hastily armed themselves and were sworn as special constables. But they gave in to the rioters without a fight, and the latter repeated the sacking and levies which had taken place at Littleport. This developed into a drunken riot.

The rioters had no clear idea of what they wanted and their chief demand was "the price of a stone of flour a day." A military force was sent for, but the rioters retreated to Littleport, and a few made a stand against the troops who hunted the fens to capture them.

As soon as the Littleport rioters had been rounded up, eighty of them were tried by a Special Commission set up by the bishop and five of them were hanged. Five others were sentenced to transportation for life and the remainder suffered various terms of imprisonment.

There was a service of thanksgiving in the Cathedral which was attended by Bishop Sparke, the last Bishop of Ely to exercise civil jurisdiction over the Isle of Ely. His butler walked in front of him bearing the sword of state, and fifty of the leading citizens accompanied him bearing white wands. Three hundred of these wand-bearers were needed to keep order among the crowd of sympathizers at the execution of the unfortunate men.   Difficulty was experienced in finding anyone willing to supply a cart to take them to their place of execution, and in the end the bishop had to pay five guineas for one.   A tablet to the memory of these five men can be seen on the south wall of the tower of St. Mary's Church.   The inscription ends with the sentence, "Let their awful fate be a warning to others."

Bishop Sparke was buried in Bishop West's Chapel together with the sword of state, now obsolete as a result of the Act passed in 1836 depriving the bishops of their civil power.   It is probably because Ely was ruled in civil affairs by bishops that it never became a borough with a mayor and corporation, though smaller towns attained that status long ago, often by extorting a charter from their overlord in return for a loan advanced by the citizens.   In Ely the wealth of the monastery and bishopric made such a course un-necessary, and it is doubtful whether the citizens were sufficiently prosperous to buy their freedom in this way.

Very few names have been handed down from the past and then only by accident.   The records upon which we have to rely for information about the non-ecclesiastical residents in Ely are the bishop's records which are housed in the Registry, formerly the gaol, which was "rebuilt and made very strong and com-modious" by Bishop Matthias Mawson about 1750.   It is the yellow brick building standing at the junction of Market Street, formerly known as Gaol Street, and Lynn Road.   Other sources of information are the documents dealing with the sale and purchase of property by the monks; besides other account rolls of the monastery.   None of these sources of information is com-plete but diligent searching often gives a clue to the history of some old Ely family.   From the time of the Littleport Riots onwards we have information and the names of most Ely residents.

Eighteen years after the Riots there was an outbreak of rick-burning in the district because of further dissatisfaction among the peasantry.   It is known, however, that ricks were sometimes set on fire by members of the fire brigades who were supposed to extinguish them, the object being to give themselves a job and the accompanying pay.

An incident involving German troops occurred at Ely in 1809, and was the cause of the political writer, William Cobbett, being fined £1,000 and serving two years' imprisonment.   Five men of the local militia, who had been ringleaders of a mutiny protesting against a stoppage of pay for their knapsacks, were sentenced to five hundred lashes each.   The mutiny had been quelled by four squadrons of German cavalry stationed at Bury, and Cobbett commented on the circumstances strongly in his *Weekly Register*. He was prosecuted for libel by the Government some time later, with the afore-mentioned result.

The flogging incident was not William Cobbett's only connection with Ely. In his famous book, *Rural Rides*, we find that he visited Ely on Thursday, 25th March, 1830. His comments are very interesting, but too long to be quoted in full. The following are some of his more important remarks: "Arrived at Ely, I first walked round the beautiful cathedral, that honour to our Catholic forefathers, and that standing disgrace to our Protestant selves. It is impossible to look at that magnificent pile without *feeling* that we are a fallen race of men . . . . Ely is what one may call a miserable little town, very prettily situated, but poor and mean."

Notice how Cobbett's description of the building tallies with that of Defoe and Byng quoted earlier in this book. "This famous building, the cathedral, is in a state of disgraceful irrepair and disfigurement. The great and magnificent windows to the east have been shortened at the bottom, and the space plastered up with brick and mortar in a very slovenly manner for the purpose of saving the expense of keeping the glass in repair. Great numbers of the windows in the upper part of the building have beeen partly closed up in the same manner, and others quite closed up."

Cobbett visited the spot where the flogging had taken place and then looked for an opportunity to talk politics to the local people. It was market day, so he went to the White Hart Inn in the Market Place, where he found the farmers had finished their market dinner—always a feature in country inns until the general use of cars and buses in the past forty years. Cobbett talked to the farmers, telling them of the circumstances of the flogging and went on to tell them that a cure for their agricultural depression would be a better system of representation in Parliament. He explained how the poor relief system had become necessary through the dissolution of the monasteries, which had formerly cared for the poor, and advised the farmers to treat their labourers fairly.

Soon after Cobbett's visit to Ely the depression came to an end with the creation of a new industry. It was discovered that certain kinds of fossils called coprolites were good for manure and that Cambridgeshire was very rich in them. A great deal of labour was required in digging for these fossils and wages went up, as did the price of land, which sometimes fetched £150 per acre.

It was at this time that the population of Ely was greater than it ever has been before or since, until the outbreak of the 1939-45 war. The census figures for the period are as follows: 1801, 3,948;

THE CATHEDRAL FROM ST. MARY'S GREEN

Plate 19

*Plate* 20                               QUAY WALK

*Plate* 21                           THE PUBLIC LIBRARY

1841, 7,041; 1871, 9,805; 1891, 8,689. The population has remained steady for about forty years at about the last figure.

Another factor which increased the prosperity of Ely at this time was the building of the railway. The Eastern Counties Railway main line from London to Norwich *via* Ely was opened on 30th July, 1845, the line to March and Peterborough in the following year, and the line to King's Lynn in 1847. In the early days of the railways they suffered from financial difficulties and at one time the Eastern Counties Railway had to hire its own locomotives from its creditors who had seized them in distraint. In 1923 the railways serving East Anglia became part of the London & North Eastern Railway Company.

CHAPTER XIV

# The Great Revival

To get a good picture of life in a cathedral city in early Victorian England one should read the "Barchester" series of novels by Anthony Trollope, commencing with *The Warden*. Although in many ways Barchester, which is an imaginary city, differs from Ely, the picture will be a fairly true one of life in the College, the Palace, and ecclesiastical circles generally. Even to-day it is possible to identify the types so vividly portrayed in these fascinating books.

One thing which must have dominated life in the College at Ely during this period is missing in the "Barchester" books, namely the restoration of the Cathedral. Ely was the first great cathedral to be thoroughly restored. The work began in 1845 under Dean Peacock, and continued for nearly thirty years under the guidance of Sir G. Gilbert Scott. As we have seen from the comments of visitors to Ely during the previous century, there was much to be done and no one who sees the building to-day will deny that it was done thoroughly, and, with few exceptions, with great sympathy and taste. The chief objects of criticism are the windows, which date from the early days of the revival of stained glass manufacture, and, though pleasing to the casual visitor, are deplored by the expert.

The first work which was done during the restoration was the rebuilding of St. Catherine's Chapel. The eastern apse had completely collapsed and the south-west transept had for a long time been cut off from the rest of the building and used as a storehouse for the builders employed from time to time. Notice how regular the new work is in comparison with the old, although it faithfully follows the original design.

At the same time the interior of the west tower was opened up and the present ceiling erected. There had been a floor across the lower part of the interior of the tower on a level with the top of the door. The marks made by it on the pillars can still be seen. It was when these alterations were being made in 1845 that Mr. Basevi, the architect of the Fitzwilliam Museum at Cambridge, fell through one of the upper floors and was killed. Before this lower floor was inserted there had been a plaster vault at the top of the great arches. When these arches were inserted in the 15th century provision for a vaulted ceiling was made; the springing stones can just be seen at the junction of the arches. Nothing appears to have been done until the above-mentioned plaster vault was inserted by Bishop Yorke in 1800.

Another of the earlier works of restoration was the removal of the choir stalls from the extreme east end of the Presbytery, where they had been placed a century before, to their present position. They had been painted in 1823 and this paint was removed. The carved panels above the stalls depicting scenes from the Old Testament, on the south side, and from the New Testament, on the north side, were added at this time. They cost £18 each and were given by individual donors. Most of the panels were carved by M. Abeloos of Louvain. The screen was made from the designs of Sir G. Gilbert Scott. In 1851 the organ was remodelled, enlarged, and removed to its present position, in a case also of Scott's design. In Scott's *Personal and Professional Recollections* he says "I placed the organ partly in the triforium and partly overhanging the choir, founding its design upon those of medieval organs, e.g. Strasburg". Before its removal the organ stood on top of a screen two bays east of the octagon.

The present screen was Scott's first introduction of an open screen into a cathedral and he relates that infinite pains went into its designing.

The restorations continued under Dean Harvey Goodwin. The most elaborate reredos to the high altar was one of the first of its type. Most of the carving was done by J. B. Philip and the colouring by Mr. Hudson of South Kensington Museum and the mosaics by a Mr. Field. A comment by Rev. B. J. Armstrong, Vicar of East Dereham, in his Diary dated 11th August, 1857 shows the change which had taken place in the Cathedral since the adverse comments by visitors at the beginning of the century—"Since I last saw it the reredos and east windows have been put it. The former is said to be the finest work of art in Europe. There is surely no Cathedral in England which surpasses Ely." The remark about the reredos should be a sobering thought to artists of the 20th century whose work is being acclaimed now!

The Lantern was restored as a memorial to Dean Peacock. Small peacocks are incorporated in the design of the eight windows which form the lantern. The top of the stonework of the Octagon had hitherto been left level, but now the pinnacles were added, improving its appearance, and probably completing the original design. The lead work of the Lantern itself was entirely remodelled with a fresh design, the corner posts terminating with turret-like tops instead of the pointed pinnacles they had borne since the reconstruction by Mr. Essex a hundred years before.

Other work carried out during the second decade of the restoration was the repair of the west porch; the securing of the foundations of the south choir aisle which were giving way; and the laying of a pavement in the nave to replace the rough stones which had previously covered the floor. The repairs to the foundations had to be continued round the south transept which was also showing signs of subsiding. This was caused by the introduction of sewers in Ely which lowered the level of water in the soil.

Dean Merivale carried on the work after he became Dean in 1870. The west tower was strengthened by means of a system of iron bands and bars. Meanwhile the ceiling of the nave which had been placed beneath the hitherto exposed rafters, was being painted by Mr. Henry Styleman le Strange, of Hunstanton, who died before he could complete the work. It was finished by Mr. Gambier Parry, who also painted the ceiling of St. Catherine's Chapel. These paintings are in the manner of medieval roof painting in other churches, the nearest example being at Peterborough Cathedral. Parry's invention, of "spirit painting" for use in a northern climate has justified itself in the way the paintings have resisted the effects of time. Mr. le Strange based his design upon that of the ceiling of the church at Hildesheim in Germany; he also painted the ceiling of the west tower, the subject being the creation of the universe. Part of the expense was defrayed by a bequest by the late Rev. G. Millers, a Minor Canon and author of a book about the Cathedral which was published in 1834, but le Strange and Parry gave their services. Dean (later Bishop) Harvey Goodwin records in his book *Ely Gossip* that many of the faces painted were portraits. "I think that Dean Peacock figures as the prophet Isaiah: but le Strange told me that he found he could make most satisfactory prophets out of bedesmen!" The other painted decoration in the Cathedral was all done, or restored, during this period. The decoration in the north transept was done at the expense of the workmen employed upon the building. The paintings of angels round the Lantern were inserted on panels; previously the tracery had been left open.

Other fittings belonging to this period include the pulpit, lectern, font and choir gates.

The total cost of all this work was £57,053 7s. 9d. Of this sum £3,600 was contributed by the bishops of Ely and their families; £22,927 10s. 7d. by the Dean and Chapter as a corporate body, and £14,907 19s. 0d. as individuals; £1,412 1s. 0d. by officers and tradesmen of the Dean and Chapter; £365 11s. 0d. by the inhabitants of Ely; and £13,840 6s. 2d. by the general public.

In the meantime works of restoration were going on in the College buildings, particularly in those used by the Kings' School. The Porta and Prior Crauden's Chapel were restored; the former Choir School, which was opened in 1862, was built and the adjoining gateway restored, with a muniment room over it for the safe keeping of the many charters and old documents belonging to the Dean and Chapter. These other works cost £12,000, very little of which was contributed from outside sources.

This vast scheme of work rivalled the time in the 14th century when Prior Crauden and Alan of Walsingham did the original building. Other improvements were suggested at the time but have never been carried out, the only great work until recent years being the cleaning and partial restoration of the Lady Chapel in 1938. The organ has continued to be enlarged and improved so that it is one of the finest instruments in the country, while the Dean and Chapter have maintained the fabric in perfect condition until 1939 when the war prevented building work from being done.

It was not only the material side of the Church which received the attention of these great Victorian churchmen. They lived in a period known as the Anglican Revival, which produced great figures such as Cardinal Newman, Keble, Selwyn and others. Church building was going on elsewhere, but at the same time the spiritual side was being given greater significance. There was more attention paid to the seemly conduct of services, and it was considered that nothing but the best was good enough to be offered to God. We have seen that the Dean and Chapter of Ely built a new Choir School and improved the organ, and from this followed the high standard of singing which Ely has since enjoyed. New settings to the services were devised, and for many years the "Ely Confession" was fashionable all over England. In 1876 Bishop Woodford founded a Theological College at Ely for the training of priests and the present building at Barton Square was opened in 1881. It has provided a steady stream of men for the Sacred Ministry, many of whom have attained high rank in the Church of England.

While the work of restoration was going on the Cathedral produced a notable historian to whom the writer of this book is much indebted for information. He was the Rev. D. J. Stewart, at one time Sacrist, who wrote an *Architectural History of Ely Cathedral* and also transcribed part of the *Liber Eliensis*. A history of the monastery written by Thomas, a 12th century monk, the *Liber Eliensis* is the chief source of information about the Saxon and Norman periods which has come down to us. The whole book has been transcribed and edited by Dr. E. O. Blake and published in 1962 by the Royal Historical Society, thus completing Stewart's work.

# CHAPTER XV

## The Bisexcentenary of St. Etheldreda

THE culmination of the restoration work described in the previous chapter was reached with a great event in the history of the Cathedral of which we are fortunate in having a detailed record. This was the celebration of the twelve hundredth anniversary of the foundation of the Abbey by St. Etheldreda, which was combined with the celebration of the completion of the works of restoration.

On Friday, 17th October, 1873, St. Etheldreda's Day, there were special services in the Cathedral. The address in the morning was by Bishop Harold Browne, which also took the form of his farewell upon leaving the Diocese. In the afternoon at Evensong the address was given by Dean Merivale. There was a special luncheon at the Palace for the clergy of the Isle of Ely and in the evening entertainments were provided for the college officials, tenants and tradesmen at the Lamb Hotel, and for the National School managers and teachers at the Bell Hotel. The bedesmen, college servants, parents of the National School children and others were entertained at the Corn Exchange. Addresses were given by Archdeacon Emery and the Bishop.

The next day the National School children attended matins and were addressed by Canon Selwyn. In the evening there was an organ recital by Dr. Chipp, the Cathedral Organist. The programme of music used throughout the Festival is still extant.

On Sunday the Bishop preached again in the morning and in the evening, after a day of special services there was a service with the Bishop of Peterborough as preacher. At evensong at 4 p.m. there had been a vast congregation, for the festival had caught the imagination of the people.

On Monday the most interesting event was a lecture by Sir Gilbert Scott which was read by his son, Mr. G. Scott, on the architectural history of the building. This lecture was a scholarly work embodying many discoveries made during the work of restoration.

At about three o'clock there was a "sumptuous luncheon" at the Corn Exchange, given by the Dean and Chapter to a large number of guests at which there were speeches by important visitors. In the evening the Bishop and Mrs. Browne held a reception at the Palace and provided supper for six hundred guests.

On Tuesday, 21st October, there was a festival of choirs at the Cathedral. Six hundred and seventy-six singers took part, with the band of the Cambridgeshire Militia playing in the triforium. We are told that "The service throughout was astonishingly well rendered, and most impressive. The strains of a military band within the walls of the Cathedral sounded strange at first, but the music and the voices of the well-trained choristers blended strikingly, and the effect was as harmonious as it was novel."

In the course of his address on St. Etheldreda's Day, Dean Merivale stressed the great period of time over which the history of the Cathedral had extended in an unbroken line. One thousand two hundred years was a longer period than most of the great empires of the world had lasted. St. Etheldreda's work still went on, but it had changed in method according to the requirements of different periods.

This is a very brief summary of the contents of a souvenir which was edited by Dean Merivale. The full text of all the sermons and addresses are included in the souvenir together with a description of the various functions which took place. There is a full programme of the music used, both for the services and at recitals, and a record of the various works undertaken and the source of the donations which were given to pay for it. Doubtless copies are to be found in many houses in the city still, for it is a record well worth preserving.

Some of the work of restoration which has already been mentioned was not completed by the bisexcentenary and it was not till six years later, in 1879, that the pinnacles of the Octagon were finished. After that there were a few works done, all of a minor nature except some restoration work on the exterior of the Lady Chapel in 1897.

# CHAPTER XVI
## Ely in the Twentieth Century

In 1894 Dean Merivale was succeeded by Dean Stubbs, a great lover of the Cathedral, who wrote several books about it which contained verses of his own composition. He also completely revised the *Ely Cathedral Handbook* making it as complete a record of the building as could be desired by most readers. Unfortunately it has not been obtainable for many years. Another student of the Cathedral's history, who was writing at the same time, was Archdeacon Chapman, who transcribed the Sacrist Rolls, or accounts, of Alan of Walsingham's period. This type of research has been carried on more recently by the Very Reverend S. J. A. Evans, and the Reverend R. H. Gibbon, who has explored the history of seventeenth-century Ely.

Bishop Harold Browne, who retired in 1873, was followed by Bishop James Russell Woodford, who founded the Theological College which was a feature of the life of the city until recently. During term time its students added a touch of the requisite "atmosphere" of a cathedral city. Bishop Woodford is buried in Bishop West's Chapel.

Lord Alwyne Compton succeeded Bishop Woodford in 1885, and was followed by Bishop Chase, a great scholar, and Bishop White-Thomson, who died on the last day of 1933. He was followed by Bishop Bernard Heywood, and in 1941 by Harold Edward Wynn, who took up residence in the house which had served as the Deanery for many years past, but was originally the Guest Hall of the Monastery.

The Deanery was occupied for about thirty years after the elevation of Dean Stubbs to the Bishopric of Truro, by Dean Kirkpatrick, a great Hebrew scholar, whose dignified presence and delightful reading voice are still remembered in the city. He was followed in 1935 by Dean Blackburne who instituted the movement known as the Friends of Ely Cathedral which takes the place of the benefactors of the past. We have seen that great building works were undertaken by wealthy men at their own expense and that the restoration work of the last century was mainly done at the expense of the Bishop, Dean and Canons, both corporately and as individuals. Times have changed so that there are no longer wealthy individuals to make such lavish benefactions, and consequently in the future great works will have to be done by means of the small contributions of the many.

In 1938 the Lady Chapel was handed back to the Dean and Chapter by the Churchwardens of Holy Trinity Parish, in whose hands it had been since 1566. A thorough cleaning and re-furnishing was necessary and this was undertaken at the expense of the Friends aided by a Public Subscription, grants from Chapter Funds and from "The Pilgrim Trust." The work was done under the supervision of Mr. H. C. Hughes, a Cambridge architect, and took nearly a year to complete. The delicate carving in clunch stone was too soft to be brushed so it had to be vacuum cleaned. A large number of eighteenth and nineteenth century memorial tablets had been set up in almost every available position, sometimes at the expense of the original carvings, which had been hacked away, and these were all removed to less obtrusive positions. A new floor was laid, and in the course of doing so a stone coffin was discovered which was believed to be that of John de Wisbech, who built the Lady Chapel. The spot is marked with a suitable memorial. It is now easy to appreciate the beauties of the building. Money could not restore it to its original glory, for the craftsmen are not alive who could do the work in the same spirit, but at least the existing work is preserved and shown off to the best advantage.

The two chantry chapels in the Cathedral have been restored for use and furnished by two groups associated with them. The Friends who were also members of Ely Theological College restored Bishop West's Chapel in which Bishop Woodford is buried; members of Jesus College, Cambridge, restored the chapel of their founder, Bishop Alcock. Both chapels are now available for services.

The whole Cathedral was lighted by electric light at the expense of the Friends.

Reference to changes which have taken place in the city have been made in various parts of this book and need not be repeated. One or two small facts might be mentioned here. During the present century the house which used to be inhabited by Oliver Cromwell became the Vicarage. At one time it was an inn.

In 1941 after the retirement of Bishop Heywood, the Bishop's Palace became an emergency hospital and Bishop Wynn and his successors have occupied the former Deanery. Since 1946 the Palace has become a school for severely handicapped girls.

The Kings' School has been expanding and taking over a number of the old monastic buildings, some of which were used as canonry houses. The Monks' Barn has been converted into a dining hall and the former dining hall in the undercroft of the buildings in the Gallery is now the school library. There are now approximately

350 boys at the School, including 16 Cathedral Choristers, the Choir School having been closed.

The extent of the city which had remained roughly the same for centuries (see the reproduction of Speed's map of 1610 on page 42) received its first extensive enlargement in the early 1920's with the development of the New Barns Estate to the north of the city. This was followed in the 1930's by private development along Lynn Road at Orchard Estate and in the Downham Road and Vineyards areas, and to a lesser extent in Cambridge Road.

My first impression of Ely was better than that of the visitors of the 18th and early 19th centuries who have been quoted in this book. On a glorious Wednesday at the end of August 1933 I arrived at Ely at noon and walked through Ely Porta round the east end of the Cathedral and out into the High Street. It was deserted and the sense of peace and quiet after life in large cities was delightful. The shops presented the appearance which they must have borne for years—drapers with windows in which hardly a square inch was without some goods on display, butchers and fishmongers with open windows. A farmyard occupied a site in Market Street and cows went daily from it to pasture in the College. I was entertained in a leisurely fashion in a pleasant garden upon which the shadow of the Cathedral tower fell daily. As four o'clock approached the bells rang for Evensong and Lay Clerks left their shops and offices and returned to continue their work when the service finished. The timetable of the Choir School revolved round the services of Matins and Evensong which were sung daily and the Choristers were taught by two of the Minor Canons. The city became a hive of industry on Thursday, market day, and again on Saturday when people from the country for a radius of some dozen miles came in for their traditional shopping outings. There were plenty of clubs and societies for all tastes, over eighty of them in fact. Every outdoor sport was catered for, and every type of indoor entertainment or cultural activity. Owing to the close connections with the University of Cambridge the local Literary Society and similar bodies were able to hear lectures by professors and dons; and the Operatic and Musical Societies had the advantage of a number of trained singers who were, or had been in the Cathedral choir. The size of the city made it large enough to support all these activities and yet it was small enough for people to feel as if they knew nearly everyone else. There was a real community spirit. Coming from life in large cities I found it delightful, and I was also impressed by the ability of the inhabitants to organize the many and varied activities.

At the commencement of the war in 1939 Ely, like the rest of the world, closed a chapter in its history and way of life. A way of life which, in spite of the changes brought about by the war of 1914-18, still retained much that would have been familiar to previous generations.

When the war began Ely was a "reception area" and a girls' grammar school, The Central Foundation School, of Bishopsgate, London, and the Jewish Free School for boys and girls were evacuated to Ely. These schools shared accommodation with the Ely High School, Needham's School and Kings' School. They brought new interests and ideas as well as problems. The teachers joined local clubs and societies and both they and the pupils contributed much to the life of the city. Ely suffered scarcely any material damage at the hands of the German bombers, but its young men who were in the Cambridgeshire Regiment suffered imprisonment and forced labour for a long period at the hands of the Japanese after their capture at Singapore. Shortly before the war a large R.A.F. Hospital was built on the Lynn Road and this still serves the inhabitants of Ely as well as R.A.F. personnel. Everyone appeared to be engaged in some contribution to the war effort, and Italian prisoners of war provided extra labour in times of shortage. When it was all over Ely went back to normal as far as possible.

If the city had not suffered material damage as a result of the war it was soon discovered that the Cathedral had suffered indirectly from the enforced lack of attention due to restrictions on building. For years the Surveyor, Mr. S. Inskip Ladds, had made a weekly inspection of the fabric and any minor repairs were undertaken at once; while each year some major work of repair was done. In 1951 it was discovered that death watch beetle was working havoc in the Lantern, the roofs of the transepts and elsewhere in the roof and it was estimated that £60,000 would be required to repair the damage and eradicate the pest. As a result of a public appeal made by Dean Hankey, who had succeeded Dean Blackburne in 1951, this large sum was raised in five years. The roofs of the Choir and Presbytery were re-timbered and re-leaded and the roof of the Octagon as well as the Lantern were re-leaded and the timbers made sound. Insecticide was put into every worm hole which was closed with wax so that any fresh outbreak could be detected. The work was carried out by Messrs. Rattee & Kett of Cambridge under the direction of Mr. S. E. Dykes Bower.

While this restoration and repair work was going on, various other smaller works were in progress. The retro-choir behind the

High Altar which had been virtually unused since the restoration by Sir G. Gilbert Scott, was converted in 1952 into a County War Memorial Chapel dedicated to St. Etheldreda.   The Friends of the Cathedral have been responsible for a number of other works. In 1959 the Library which occupied the eastern aisle of the south transept was reduced to two thirds of its size and the southernmost bay converted into the Chapel of St. Dunstan and St. Ethelwold for use as a quiet place for private prayer.   In the 1960's under the Surveyor, Mr. Donovan Purcell, extensive restoration of the Galilee Porch was undertaken and much stone was renewed both inside and outside where the action of the weather had led to the decay of the Purbeck marble especially.   Restoration of the decaying stone pinnacles on the south side of the Lady Chapel was also begun.   Altogether the Dean and Chapter and the Friends of the Cathedral aided by a generous public have nobly lived up to the example set them by their predecessors of a hundred years ago in caring for the magnificent building entrusted to their care.   When one considers the work done in the 18th century by Mr. Essex it would appear that the middle of each century may bring similar problems.   The Cathedral now looks better cared for, not only inside and out, but in its immediate surroundings, than it has done for many years.   The churchyard on the north side has been tidied up and made pleasant and the paths and roadways in the College are maintained better than ever before.

While the work on the Cathedral has been going on there have been changes in the city itself.   One of the most striking developments has been the educational centre just outside the built-up area in Downham Road.   During 1962-3 St. Audrey's School and Ely High School were moved to an extensive site and in 1968 Needham's County Secondary School was added to the group. The Urban District Council built more houses at High Barns in 1955 and at West Fen in 1962 as well as houses for elderly people nearer the centre of the city.   There has also been development off St. John's Road, West End, Witchford Road and elsewhere. After centuries the shape of the city has changed.

The appearance of the Market Place has been altered by the removal of the Corn Exchange and the adjoining Public Room. The Corn Exchange was built in 1847 and was characteristic of a country town.   The site has been filled by a modern shopping precinct.   A new Post Office and supermarket have also helped change the character of the Market Place.   On Palace Green a modern Public Library was opened in 1966 on the site of a picturesque house known as Minster Cottage part of which dated back to the time of Queen Anne.   For many years domestic architecture in

Ely had been poor in design and it must be said that many of the most recent changes have been for the better.

The last industry mentioned in a previous chapter was the digging of coprolites. This ceased and agriculture remained the main industry. In 1925 a large Beet Sugar Factory was built at what was known in the middle ages as Turbutsea. This provides a great deal of work in the factory itself during the "campaign" which lasts from September till the New Year, and for the transport industry which conveys the beet. On the farms the cultivation and lifting of the beet was all done by hand and created a great deal of work for both men and women. Since the war machines have been perfected which will do most of this work and the manufacture of the machines themselves provides alternative employment under more pleasant conditions in Ely itself.

A factory in Brays Lane was used for canning and later for making jam; it closed in 1963 but re-opened for the manufacture of spraying equipment for farmers. Such is the way in which Ely has adapted itself to changing conditions. At one time there were two breweries, one at Quayside which was closed many years ago, and the other at Fore Hill at the end of 1968.

One of the most striking developments has been the phenominal growth of a boat building firm which also lets cruisers out on hire on similar lines to the operators on the Norfolk Broads. Over 150 boats are built each year. The river bank between Quayside and the Cutter Inn has been greatly improved with a pleasant walk and seats and presents a most attractive approach to the visitor who arrives by water. In spite of this Quayside itself retains its old-world atmosphere better than almost any other street in Ely.

The Isle of Ely has for many years been a separate administrative county, but in April 1965 it was amalgamated with Cambridgeshire to form a single County Council. Thus the last reminder of the domain of Queen Etheldreda and her successors, the Monastery and the Bishops, has been lost.

Owing to its situation surrounded by valuable farm land, Ely is not likely to be developed as a "new town". It shows every sign of maintaining its character and using the resource and enterprise of its citizens to enjoy modest prosperity. In the Cathedral it has an incomparable asset which attracts visitors from all parts of the world, a living witness to the continuity of Christianity in our land over a period of 1300 years. Not only is the building used for daily worship in the best traditions of the Church of England with excellent music, but it is the focal point of a diocese which extends over the whole of the counties of

Cambridgeshire and Huntingdonshire and part of Norfolk. Great gatherings of people meet for special services many times each year.

Smaller gatherings and entertainments not suitable for the setting provided by the Cathedral are now catered for in Ely by an imaginative scheme initiated by Watney Mann (East Anglia) Ltd., the successors to the two breweries which once flourished in the city. This firm offered the Maltings, built in 1868 for Harlock's brewery, to the Ely Urban District Council for the nominal sum of £100 on condition that the building should be converted into a public hall. Although the idea was obviously inspired by the successful conversion of the Maltings at Snape, in Suffolk, into a concert hall-cum-opera house, the Ely scheme was more modest and was intended to cater for the entertainment of the citizens of Ely itself. The result has been most successful and the building, opened in 1971, has become an asset to the city as well as continuing the revival of the Quayside, standing as it does overlooking the busy scene on the river. Since the Public Room and the Corn Exchange which once stood on the Market Place have ceased to be available for public functions, and the Central Hall in Market Street, which served in their place during the 1930's in turn was lost some time in the 1940's, there was inadequate provision in Ely for the many social activities which once took place. The Maltings now provides the facilities in an even better way than its predecessors.

The Cathedral provides a setting for secular concerts and other performances on a scale larger than the Maltings can accommodate, and of a quality which towns of similar size are not usually able to enjoy. The thirteenth centenary of the founding of the Cathedral celebrated in 1973 is an example of the type of choral and orchestral concerts, operas and mystery plays which are presented—a wider choice than the programme for the festivities one hundred years earlier which has been quoted in Chapter XV.

Another celebration took place in 1971 when the King's School marked its millenary by staging a pageant among other events. Few if any other schools in this country can claim to have been founded over 1000 years ago and to have an unbroken existence. The school is larger and more flourishing now than at any time and has taken over a number of the former monastic buildings besides the former Theological College and Needham's School in Back Hill. New buildings have also been added. As it began its second thousand years the school broke new ground by admitting girls as well as boys.

The 1960's have seen a phenomenal rise of interest by the general public in ancient buildings and in cathedrals in particular. Ely Cathedral, always an attraction to visitors from many lands, has

drawn larger and larger numbers of visitors who cannot fail to have
been impressed and, in many cases, inspired by its beauty and the
skill and devotion of its builders.    Humility is not a characteristic
of the latter part of the twentieth century, but the thought that in
what we might tend to regard as a barbarous, semi-civilized age our
ancestors were able to conceive and put into execution such an
ambitious scheme as the building of this vast church, a scheme
which could not even be attempted in the present day for lack of
financial means, ought to make the thinking visitor feel humble.
In an age when nothing is made to last, when there is a lack of
confidence in the future, rather similar to that fear which existed in
men's minds before the year 1000 A.D., this monument to man's
urge to do a job to the best of his ability so that it would last for
centuries, might well lead to a change of heart and a revival of
honest work.    It is not only a permanent material monument, but
a symbol of the eternal truths which have been taught on this spot
for thirteen centuries, truths which have survived changes of
fashion as well as the ebb and flow of faith itself.

The future looks bright for Ely and its Story is by no means
ended.

# Bibliography

*Cambridgeshire.* By NIKOLAUS PEVSNER. Buildings of England. (Penguin.) 1954.

*Highways and Byways in Cambridge and Ely.* By E. CONYBEARE. (Macmillan.) 1910.

*Cambridgeshire.* King's England Series, ed. ARTHUR MEE. (Hodder & Stoughton.) 1939.

*Magna Britannia.* Vol. II Part I Cambridgeshire. By Rev. DANIEL LYSONS and SAMUEL LYSONS. 1808.

*Medieval Fenland.* By H. C. DARBY, Ph.D. (Cambridge University Press.) 1940.

*The Draining of the Fens.* By H. C. DARBY, Ph.D. (Cambridge University Press.) 1940.

*The Cambridge Region.* Ed. by H. C. DARBY, Ph.D. (Cambridge University Press.) New edition 1968.

*A Human Geography of Cambridgeshire.* By JOHN JONES. (Sidgwick & Jackson.) 1924.

*The Place-Names of Cambridgeshire and the Isle of Ely.* By R. H. REANEY. (Cambridge University Press.) 1943.

*The Transactions of the Cambs. and Hunts. Archaeological Society.* Published annually. (Mason & Dorman.)

*The Proceedings of the Cambridge Antiquarian Society.* Published annually. (Deighton Bell.)

*The Geology of Fenland.* By S. B. J. SKERTCHLEY. 1877.

*The Victoria County History of Cambridgeshire and the Isle of Ely.* Vol. I. (Oxford University Press.) 1938.

*Handbook to the Natural History of Cambridgeshire.* By MARR and SHIPLEY. (Cambridge University Press.)

*Fenland, Past and Present.* By MILLER and SKERTCHLEY. 1878.

*Handbook to Ely Cathedral.* By DEAN STUBBS. (Tyndall.)

*A Description of the Cathedral Church of Ely.* By G. MILLERS. 2nd Ed. (J. White.) 1808.

*Architectural History of Ely Cathedral.* By D. J. STEWART. (Van Voorst.) 1868.

*The Monastery of Ely.* By S. INSKIP LADDS. (Tyndall.)

*The Sacrist Rolls of Ely.* By Archdeacon F. R. CHAPMAN. 2 Vols. (Published privately.) 1907.

*An Architectural History of the Benedictine Monastery of St. Etheldreda at Ely.* By T. D. ATKINSON. (Cambridge University Press.) 1933.

*The History and Antiquities of the Conventual and Cathedral Church of Ely.* By JAMES BENTHAM. 1771.

*The Sculptures in the Lady Chapel at Ely.* By M. R. JAMES. (Nutt.) 1895.

*The Roof Bosses in Ely Cathedral.* By C. J. P. CAVE. (Friends of Ely Cathedral.)

*Report on the Windows of Ely Cathedral.* By Canon E. MILNER WHITE. (Friends of Ely Cathedral.)

*A Description of the Sextry Barn at Ely.* By R. WILLIS. (Camb. Antiq. Soc.) 1843.

*Liber Eliensis.* By THOMAS, a Monk of the Convent in the 12th century. Books I and II transcribed by Canon D. J. STEWART. (Anglia Christiana Society.) 1848.

*Liber Eliensis.* Ed. for the Royal Historical Society by E. O. BLAKE, Ph.D. Camden third series. Vol. XCII. (Royal Hist. Soc.) 1962.

*Anglia Sacra.* By HENRY WHARTON. 1691.

*Survey of the Cathedrals.* By BROWNE WILLIS. 1730.

*Handbook to the Eastern Cathedrals.* By R. J. KING. (John Murray.) 1862.